Eighty
Adventurous Years

AN AUTOBIOGRAPHY

Books by Sherwood Eddy

❦

MY SILVER AND GOLD—1897
INDIA AWAKENING—1911
THE NEW ERA IN ASIA—1913
THE STUDENTS OF ASIA—1915
SUFFERING AND THE WAR—1916
WITH OUR SOLDIERS IN FRANCE—1917
THE RIGHT TO FIGHT—1918
EVERYBODY'S WORLD—1920
FACING THE CRISIS—1922
THE NEW WORLD OF LABOR—1923
THE ABOLITION OF WAR—1924
(with Kirby Page)
NEW CHALLENGES TO FAITH—1926
MAKERS OF FREEDOM—1926
(with Kirby Page)
RELIGION AND SOCIAL JUSTICE—1927
SEX AND YOUTH—1928
AM I GETTING AN EDUCATION?—1929
(in part)
THE CHALLENGE OF RUSSIA—1931
THE CHALLENGE OF THE EAST—1931
THE WORLD'S DANGER ZONE—1932
THE CHALLENGE OF EUROPE—1933
A PILGRIMAGE OF IDEAS—1934
RUSSIA TODAY—1934
EUROPE TODAY—1937
CREATIVE PIONEERS—1937
(with Kirby Page)
REVOLUTIONARY CHRISTIANITY—1939
I HAVE SEEN GOD DO IT—1939
THE KINGDOM OF GOD AND THE AMERICAN DREAM—1941
MAKER OF MEN—1941
MAN DISCOVERS GOD—1942
A PORTRAIT OF JESUS—1943
A CENTURY WITH YOUTH—1944
I HAVE SEEN GOD WORK IN CHINA—1944
PATHFINDERS OF THE WORLD MISSIONARY CRUSADE—1945
GOD IN HISTORY—1947
YOU WILL SURVIVE AFTER DEATH—1950
EIGHTY ADVENTUROUS YEARS—1955

Eighty Adventurous Years

AN AUTOBIOGRAPHY

SHERWOOD EDDY

Harper & Brothers   Publishers

NEW YORK

To Louise

Contents

❧

Introduction

BY REINHOLD NIEBUHR

In writing an introduction for Sherwood Eddy's autobiography I must resist the temptation of being too
personal in emphasizing what he has meant to me. Yet I
must gratefully acknowledge the profound influence he
has had on my life. We became acquainted on one of the
European tours which he conducted after the First World
War. After that he enlisted me as a helper in his tour of
the colleges and insisted on paying the salary of an assistant minister for my parish to free me for college work.
Subsequently he was instrumental in bringing me to the
faculty of Union Seminary.

But while he thus influenced the course of my career,
he more profoundly influenced me by the power and graciousness of a wholly dedicated life. Sherwood Eddy has
frequently been described by our European friends as
"typically American"; but he has this at least in common
with all typical people: he is thoroughly unique and no
one else in America could be found to compare with him.
I suppose his energy is typically American, at least from
the perspective of Europe; and so was his sublime directness with which he approached complicated issues. But
there is a highly unique combination of qualities and interests in the man which would mark him out in any culture
or any age.

9

He was first of all a missionary and evangelist; and all of his subsequent interests could not dampen his missionary zeal and evangelistic enthusiasm. He is a Christian of simple and gracious faith; but his orthodoxy has never hardened or made him inhospitable to new winds of doctrine. His passion for social justice embodied the best in the tradition of the social gospel and frequently prompted him to play the part of the prophet standing before the king, whether in Hitler's Germany or in the China of Chiang Kai-shek. He added to his vocation as missionary evangelist a tireless interest in the religious life of our college students. He conducted more college missions than any other living Christian leader. In addition, for decades he conducted a series of European seminars, because he was rightly concerned that Americans should understand the responsibilities of our power in a world of revolutionary and military upheavals.

I know of no one who, having detected a need, would proceed so directly to meet it and who would be so sensitive to unfilled needs on the various levels of life, social and political, religious or international. This directness of approach, coupled with a remarkable humility of spirit which positively invited criticism of even his dearest enterprises and interests, made him an original force in any project he undertook. I could enumerate at least a dozen enterprises in which Sherwood Eddy gave leadership, and enlisted the services of men who were probably intellectually his superiors but who were the willing followers of his leadership and the grateful beneficiaries of his uncomplicated directness.

I am glad that in these pages he has thrown some light

upon the influence of his remarkable mother on his life. One winter when Sherwood's current "project" was bringing the knowledge of birth control to poor people everywhere, but especially to the people in India, his mother was present at a meeting in International House, New York, at which he sought to arouse enthusiasm for this project. His mother, who had some of the formidable directness and a courage which explained his own, stormed out of this particular meeting muttering, "I don't believe a word of it." She followed the career of her son with loving pride, but when he espoused this new doctrine she was not loath to challenge him publicly.

Sherwood Eddy's career is proof of the tremendous good which a wholly dedicated life can accomplish. It is also a reminder that the evangelical experience, cultivated by the pietistic movement of which Sherwood's life was a fruit, need not result in purely individualistic goodness. Such goodness is afraid of, and ineffective in, the complicated ethical problems produced in such profusion by a technical civilization. Eddy exhibits many of the graces of a truly Christian life, but the quality that entitles him most to the gratitude of our generation is the combination of a warm personal piety and a passion for justice in all the wider relations of life in which such piety usually loses its original force.

The traditional exponents of the "social gospel" usually exhausted their message in ethical and social teaching, which had little of the "Gospel" in it, while the older piety tended to be ineffective, and sometimes positively reactionary, in meeting any social or political issue. Mr. Eddy is a vivid reminder to us all that evangelical experience and social passion can be united. In that sense he has been a reincarnation of the spirit of Hebrew prophetism, always inquiring after "the word of the Lord" and ready to proclaim it against the pride and prejudices of men.

REINHOLD NIEBUHR

Foreword

On my eighty-fourth birthday, January 19, 1955, I approach the close of my thirty-sixth book, my autobiography. Now certain kinds of people are expected to write autobiography—the scholar, for instance, or the statesman or the saint. I belong to none of these categories, but I have had the unique experience of working for sixty years in thirty countries over four continents. These six decades spanned an unprecedented "time of troubles," a period of world wars and revolutions, culminating in a new atomic age. What a time in which to live! Perhaps I may be indulged in reminiscence.

In the Orient I had the priceless privilege of living in the homes of Gandhi and Nehru during India's long and bloodless revolution. For twenty years I watched China's rising nationalism. Fifteen times my work took me to Russia. I knew the country under the Czars; then under Lenin and Stalin I saw it become a totalitarian police state behind an iron curtain and finally begin its campaign for world conquest. I desire to bear witness to some of the forces I have seen at work in six decades in Asia, Europe, and America, for I am one of the last active members of an older generation now rapidly passing.

As I look back upon life it seems one glorious adventure. From early boyhood days of camping in what we loved to think of as the "wild West," to shooting elephant and tiger in the jungles of my own mission station in India, and on into that bigger and greater hunt for men, life has seemed one long adventure. During it all I have often been overwhelmed by opportunities far beyond my limited abilities, but learning to know the Power that helps to make possible the impossible has been one of the greatest adventures.

One reward of incessant travel has been the privilege of knowing so many glorious people in the world. I have been blessed with undeserved friendships. As proof of such friendship I am especially indebted to three friends for their criticism of this manuscript. There is my dear friend Reinhold Niebuhr, whose fine thinking stimulates me and whose undeserved Introduction I gratefully appreciate. Dr. A. T. Mollegen of Alexandria, Virginia, Theological Seminary has made many suggestions and wisely corrected some of the statements in my heresies, especially in the chapter, "What I Believe." More still I am indebted to my friend and fellow worker for more than forty years, Kirby Page, who has patiently reviewed all my previous printed material—books, pamphlets, and several hundred report letters covering a period of fifty-eight years, loaned from the archives of the Yale library. I am also indebted to my publishers, who have been patient with revision of this manuscript. Most of all, throughout the whole book, as in all areas of my life, I am indebted to my wife and have accordingly dedicated the book to her.

SHERWOOD EDDY

Jacksonville, Illinois
January 19, 1955

Eighty
Adventurous Years

AN AUTOBIOGRAPHY

Chapter 1

❦

EARLY YEARS OF ADVENTURE

I was born in Leavenworth, Kansas, January 19, 1871. Not only the West but the wild West was in my blood. Fort Leavenworth was long the base from which the Indian wars were waged against the retreating Sioux, and I used to buy bows and arrows from Indian boys who were members of tribes that were brought into the Fort. Before my advent, herds of buffalo had roamed over the adjacent plains and two of our neighbors had made fortunes out of buffalo hides, some of which we still used as lap robes on sleigh rides. My mother had gone to school with Buffalo Bill Cody, who stayed in school only long enough to learn to write his name because he had to assume the support of the family when his father was killed, and hence took to scouting in the Indian wars as a means of livelihood.

In those days Leavenworth was on the border between the North and South as well as between the East and West. From 1854 to 1857 Northerners and Southerners had fought for the possession of "bleeding Kansas." Psychologically the fight over slavery continued for many years, with Leavenworth the center of the proslavery faction and the adjacent town of Lawrence the center of the free-state settlers. Mobs were free with tar and feathers; there was violence and shooting and an occasional hanging.

The headquarters of the southern proslavery party was in a hotel which was rented from my grandfather. It stood next to his house, and my mother remembered seeing the belle of Leavenworth offer a bouquet to a freshly arrived contingent of Alabama and Missouri men if one of them would bring in a free-state man's scalp. The flame of hatred was fanned by the act of a proslavery captain, Emory, who ordered a drunken German settler to halt and when the man did not obey, shot and killed him, leaving his wife and three children without a provider. My grandmother so indignantly criticized this act of violence that her whole family was ordered to leave town on the first Missouri River steamboat, along with several other pro-free-state citizens. Some left on the boat as ordered, others escaped to near-by Fort Leavenworth, but my mother's family closed up their house and remained inside, hiding for some weeks, while my grandfather went out each night under cover of darkness to procure food.

My father's family was of Pilgrim ancestry, descendants of John Alden and Priscilla, and of Samuel Eddy, who arrived in America in 1630 in the third Pilgrim ship, *Handmaid*, after twelve stormy weeks at sea. Governor Winthrop records that the master of the ship "came to Boston with Captain Standish and two gentlemen passengers," the brothers Samuel and John Eddy, who were sons of William Eddy, vicar of Cranbrook near Canterbury. With them they brought the family coat of arms, which displayed a sword and a cross and bore the motto: "The cross is to me a welcome rest." Both symbols, sword and cross, became dominant in my life.

Certain scions of the Eddy family moved westward, and

at the time of my birth my father, George A. Eddy, was a wholesale druggist and one of the successful businessmen of Leavenworth. An outstanding citizen, he assumed leadership in various reform movements against the saloon, commercialized vice, and organized crime. Because he refused to sell liquor, as was customarily done by wholesale druggists, he lost some ten thousand dollars annual income. In 1889 he was appointed one of the two receivers of the Missouri, Kansas and Texas Railway by his friend Judge Brewer, after whom my youngest brother was named. The judge later became Justice of the Supreme Court of the United States. My father proved to be a capable executive and helped to restore the railroad to solvency. He was a reserved, quiet-spoken man, thoughtful, kindly, and efficient, with a wholesome and enduring influence on all of us.

In the summer of 1889 I began to travel with my father in his private railway car, "The Prairie Queen," and I sailed my catboat on the Atlantic, the Pacific, the Great Lakes, and the Gulf of Mexico. Without any conscious choice of my own I have been moving about on the continents and across the oceans ever since. At times my life has appeared to be a series of fortuitous experiences, but as I look back over the fourscore years there seems to have been a pattern working toward a finished design. I conceive all history as the joint work of God and man. I think of God's eternal purpose as the warp and of man's brief, broken, and rebellious handiwork as the cross threads, the woof. Hegel dares to say, "What has happened, and is happening every day, is not only not 'without God' but is essentially His work."

My mother, Margaret Louise Eddy, was the dynamic

and decisive member of our household. Indeed, she was one of the most amazing persons I have known, and remained unique and refreshing until her death at eighty-six. To my mother I owe almost every trait that is mine: I inherited her characteristics, including her limitations. Although born in New York State, my mother grew up in the early days of the wild and lawless West. Her father, Miles Norton, died when she was ten years old, and she soon had to fend for herself and help support the family. Because she had a timid mother she became not only self-reliant and aggressive but somewhat headstrong and undisciplined. Her critical faculty was keen and overdeveloped. Throughout her life she had an indomitable will, an open, restless mind, a love of good reading, a thirst for knowledge, and a passion for moral reform. She was of the stuff of which reformers are made, as well as martyrs and fanatics. Had she remained a single woman she would have joined in the crusades led by her contemporaries, Susan B. Anthony and Frances Willard, but she believed a married woman's place was with her family—although she certainly never confined her interests within four walls.

At the age of fourteen she entered Elmira College, in reality an academy, in New York. She reveled in Latin and mathematics, as none of her sons ever did. In college she was the leader of the opposition in a revolt against the unwholesome "self-reporting" system then in vogue. Later she got the girls to go on strike and refuse the loathsome dried fish in their weekly diet. When the college continued to serve it she organized a band to break into the cellar and roll the barrels of fish down into the lake.

At the age of sixteen she returned to Kansas to support

her family by teaching. She asked for her first month's salary in forty one-dollar bills, which she proudly took home to her mother. Although young men older than herself were among her pupils she was a strict disciplinarian and a stimulating teacher. After three and a half years of teaching she had saved enough money to enter one of the first classes of Vassar College but she was compelled to leave before graduation because of agonizing headaches caused by astigmatic vision, for which corrective glasses were then unobtainable.

This overintellectual schoolteacher who knew nothing of housework and had never seen a young baby became my mother. The day after my arrival, a driveling little red shrimp, my mother was found weeping uncontrollably because she was sure her son was an idiot and that the family was trying to hide the fact from her. There have been moments in my later life when I—and doubtless others as well—have suspected that my mother was right in her first estimate.

My mother made a host of friends wherever she went, but she never lost her zeal for teaching and reform; her most distinguishing trait was her terrific moral earnestness. Our home was an open forum of free speech. No one, whether parent or child, was sacrosanct or above criticism. We were taught loyalty to principles rather than to persons. No one in our house was ever in danger of being spoiled by the praise of a doting mother. There was a continual stirring of the eagle's nest to crowd the young into forced flight.

I look upon my mother with admiration and amazement, but I have never been permitted to be unmindful of her faults or of my own. I choose, however, to dwell upon her strengths. When she came out to visit us in India she saw the need for a school for the children of the missionaries and other foreigners. With undaunted initiative she returned to America alone and raised the money to start this school at Kodaikanal, South India. Here, too, she was an able teacher and prepared her pupils to enter college with flying colors, especially in mathematics and Latin. When over seventy she went off for a ten days' trip to study the wild flowers of New England with all the enthusiasm of her college days. A little later she said she was ashamed she had never studied Karl Marx and she would like to begin if I would bring her his books.

I was not a rugged child. A "blue baby" at birth, I continued to be sickly. At the age of five I contracted scarlet fever from my little sister, who died at that time. Scarlet fever was followed by measles and then whoopng cough. At one time I was supposed to be dying; three doctors had given me up; I refused all nourishment; but at almost the last gasp I said there was one thing I would eat—buckwheat cakes! And I have been fond of them ever since. During those months of illness I gazed out of my sickroom window, across countless medicine bottles, envious of the big boy across the street who was building a boat to launch on the near-by Missouri River. This hero, Fred Whitrock, later became a train robber of incredible audacity, ambitious to take his place with Jesse James and Billy the Kid. I continued to be a timid little chap and was always reminded by the stronger, rougher boys that I was likely to drop dead of heart failure at any moment. Fortunately for me I had one playmate who was a big bully, ready upon the slightest provocation to "lick the tar" out of my sickly self. One day in self-defense and desperation I scratched the skin off his face, thereby gaining self-confidence while he as suddenly lost his zest for fighting.

I fought my way to health and in later boyhood was an outdoor extrovert, supremely healthy and happy, with no morbid tensions or complexes. We boys played scouts and Indians, and later, in high school, camping and shooting were the supreme delights of my days. Our expeditions in covered wagons had all the excitement of a Columbus voyage. As the artist of the gang I used to paint "Pike's Peak or Bust," or "Pawnee Bill's Wild West Show" on our westward-rolling wagons. On these expeditions we had our baseball nine, our musical instruments, and above all our shotguns to provide meat—quail, rabbits, and squirrels.

One night when our horses got loose I went with Tom Harker, the toughest member of the gang, to catch them and fasten them up again. When we returned to the tent and I found the other boys sleeping I asked Tom to pass me his big ten-bore shotgun. I poked it out of the tent and fired into the dead stillness of the night. Our badly frightened tentmates, awakened so abruptly, assumed that we were being attacked. That afternoon there had been a tramp around our camp and the boy next to whose head I had fired the gun said he saw a flash of gunfire from the woods. The only two boys brave enough to rush out and face the enemy were Tom Harker and myself. Ah, those were the days! This camping out and learning to shoot was of more importance than I realized and in later years in India served me well when my doctor ordered hunting expeditions to help me regain my health.

In addition to the democratic nature of our family life we were influenced by the local Congregational church with its liberal and stimulating New England heritage. As we grew older we were nurtured on Henry Drummond and Lyman Abbott and minds of like caliber. I was the oldest child, Dana was next, and Brewer the youngest. Dana grew to manhood, married Katherine Willard, prepared himself at Yale and Johns Hopkins to be a medical missionary, but died shortly after his graduation. Brewer went to Yale, was active in the famous Yale missionary band, married Josephine Russell, and finally became a secretary to the American Board of Commissioners for Foreign Missions of the Congregational Church, serving in that capacity until his death in 1946.

From Leavenworth high school I went to Phillips Andover Academy. I had serious trouble with my eyes due to glasses which did not correct my astigmatism. Because of this difficulty I took the scientific course, which then demanded less reading than the classical studies, and followed engineering in the Sheffield Scientific School at Yale, from which I was graduated in 1891. My grades were quite mediocre; I stood sixth in high school, third in Phillips Andover, and halfway down the class at Yale; as yet I had found no object or mission in life to call forth serious effort.

In college I had a thoroughly good time with athletics, proms and parties, sleighing and skating, and general hilarity. Our suite, shared by four freshmen, was filled with stolen signs and notices, such as, "Gentlemen will not, others must not, spit on the floor." My landlady reported me to the faculty for misdemeanors. An old scrapbook lies before me now with its scores of souvenirs recalling rollicking times: samples of clothing torn from students during class rushes, souvenirs of hazing, of April Fools' jokes, of athletic victories, and youthful "best girls."

Innocent of any future pacifism, as a Yale senior I wrote a military essay for which I won a prize of twenty-five dollars. I took military drill under Captain Totten and gave no more thought to it than did the nitwit classmate beside me. Captain Totten not only lectured on military strategy but also on the Anglo-Saxon race as the survivors of the lost Ten Tribes of Israel. He made thrilling prophecies as to the millennial end of the age. We were soon to be "caught up into the air," and the date was "nearer than 1899." We were in the class of '91!

I do not wish to disparage the value of these lectures or my own proficiency in military tactics, my diploma volunteered the information: "The prize Military Essayist of his class. . . . *In time of need his services will be of value.*" (The italics are mine!) As I recall them the lectures on the millennium and those on military training were of equal value. Many years later I received a very striking confirmation of Captain Totten's prophecies on an old Assyrian tablet of 2800 B.C. It read, "Our earth is degenerate in these later days. There are signs that the world is speedily coming to an end. Children no longer obey their parents. Every man wants to write a book. The end of the world is evidently approaching."

As I look back upon my college years there are a few things for which I am thankful. I kept morally straight and I decided against joining a fraternity. Also I stumbled upon an anthology of poetry entitled, *With the Poets*,

edited by Canon Farrar. I idly began to read "Adam and
Eve's Morning Hymn" from Milton's *Paradise Lost*, when
the mental scales suddenly fell from my eyes. My heart
leaped to the cadence and mighty ground swell of the
majestic Milton. I read on through Shelley, Keats, Words-
worth, Tennyson, and Browning. Here was life and I was
avid for it! The habit of good reading was formed for life.

The supreme adventure of my life at Yale was the result
of an apparently chance conversation with a classmate
who was planning to attend the Northfield Student Conference. "Why don't you go with us?" he asked. I thanked
him but turned down the invitation. Why should I go to
Northfield? But my fellow student was so eagerly antici-
pating the conference that his enthusiasm showed in his
voice as he told me that Henry Drummond was coming
from Scotland to join the American leaders. According to
my friend I would gain a lot by going—a great uplift, a
personal blessing, a sense of direction. I told him I wanted
no uplift, no blessing and that I knew where I was going.

Then he got down to my level and mentioned the tennis,
baseball, swimming and dancing of the Yale delegation.
"Do you mean to say you really have a good time?" I
asked. "You bet we do!" he replied. "All right, I'll go.
You can have the blessing and I'll take the good time."

I dropped into a back seat at the first meeting, hoping
that it would soon be over and I could get out for tennis.
Then Dwight L. Moody, huge and homely, rose to speak.
He was the most dynamic human being I had ever met—
terribly in earnest. I remember his text: "If any man thirst,
let him come and drink. From within him shall flow
rivers." As Moody spoke I began to see myself, a college

student, cold, selfish, cynical, sneering at the poor boys, "the muckers" from the factories and slums of the college town. There was I, so hypercritical that a fellow student had been warned not to room with me because of the effect it might have on him. As Moody spoke I began to realize that I was sinful—I knew what the word meant as I had never known before. Moody did not accuse me; he simply held up a picture of the abundant life, the dedicated life, such as I had never visualized, before which I felt shriveled in selfishness.

Before he had finished I saw myself as I was—no good to my college, to my country, to man, or to God. I also saw Moody as he was, an uneducated man using bad grammar, but under God shaking the continent of America as he had moved the colleges and cities of Great Britain. A great thirst sprang up in my heart. Oh for a man to rise in me, that the man I was might cease to be! That night I forgot all about my "good time." I went out into the field and by a great rock I wrestled with my own selfishness and sin. That night marked a turning point in my life. God became forever real to me. Religion was no longer a tradition or a secondhand experience inherited from my elders.

My classmate had been right; the direction of my life was changed. I was soon teaching a Bible class of students under the direction of James McConaughy, and out of this work came the invitation, a few months later, to join the staff of the Twenty-third Street Branch of the YMCA in New York City. Thus it happened that after leaving Yale I spent a year in New York and for the first time came in touch with life in the raw. My previous experiences had all been with respectable people in small-town or college communities. Now I was introduced to the problems of a big city; I had to deal with the unemployed, the dissolute, the men who had failed to make the grade. My room was just below that of Robert R. McBurney, the ideal YMCA secretary with a genius for friendship. Intimate contact with him would alone have been worth my year on the job.

The experiences of those months in New York revolutionized my life plans. I had intended to go into the lumber business and make money—plenty of it, for I believed that money was power. Now I was faced with two questions which I could not escape. Where in the world was the greatest spiritual need? Where was the greatest opportunity for service? In searching for the answers I was led to a decision to become a foreign missionary in the needier half of the world, and the next year while at Union Theological Seminary I signed the declaration card of the Student Volunteer Movement. My lifework henceforth would be the making of men instead of money.

In preparation for overseas work I spent two years at Union Theological Seminary in New York working as student assistant to the great preacher Dr. Charles H. Parkhurst, during the time that he was launching his bold attacks on the graft and crime of Tammany Hall. With my two Yale classmates as roommates, Henry Luce (father of the publisher) and Horace Pitkin, I spent week ends in New England colleges on deputation work for the Student Volunteer Movement. Before my final year at Princeton Theological Seminary, which I attended after Union, I spent one year as a secretary for the Volunteer Movement, as did Luce and Pitkin, Luce visiting the colleges of the

South, Pitkin campuses of the Middle West, and I the colleges of the East and Canada.

It is difficult for this generation of students to realize how impelling was the appeal of the Volunteer Movement for us in those days. The simple declaration read: "It is my purpose if God permit to become a foreign missionary." It was a pledge not easily made or lightly taken. As Student Volunteer bands were formed on the campuses they often proved to be revitalizing units for all college life. Schools began to think in terms of the number of their students who were seriously preparing for life in China, Japan, Africa—all parts of the world. The Volunteers found they needed to explore all areas of community life and resources as well as to tap the wells of spiritual power. College days for us students were enriched with the constant picture of the future, "when we are on the field." Forty countries in the world were calling for volunteers, and "the evangelization of the world in this generation" was accepted as a personal responsibility. We student volunteers went out not to destroy but to fulfill, to build upon the rich heritage of each country's past in order to produce a better future. We went out with a ministry of healing, of education, of scientific agriculture, of better living conditions; we went to relieve misery, want, and famine. We went to heal broken bodies, dwarfed minds, and wounded spirits.

As Luce and I prepared ourselves during our last year at Princeton we began every day at five in the morning, spending the first hour in thorough Bible study and the second hour in prayer, each in his own room. Those two unhurried hours in devotions each morning changed the texture of our lives. We experienced joy unbroken throughout each day. The word of MacKay of Uganda was with us constantly: "I must be more terribly in earnest where I am, knowing that I must so soon go elsewhere." We omitted the heavy Sunday dinner that we might have clear minds for reading, thought, and prayer. We must become new men if, under God, we had a world to win. We shared the feeling that must have been experienced by Ignatius Loyola and Francis Xavier when as students they prayed and prepared for their lifework, or as did the Wesleys and Whitefield in Oxford.

In the winter of 1896 I made my third trip across the Atlantic to attend the Student Volunteer Convention in Liverpool, where I was to speak. On the first day of January just as we were nearing the end of the voyage, our ship, the Cunard *Cephalonia*, ran on the rocks and went down off South Stack Lighthouse near Holyhead, Wales. Fortunately all the passengers got off in lifeboats and were rescued. My first shipwreck was a thrilling adventure and perhaps presaged some of the stormy experiences that would combine excitement and fulfillment during the many years ahead of me.

Chapter 2

✿

FIFTEEN YEARS IN INDIA

Horace Pitkin, Henry Luce, and I had planned to spend our lives in China, but at the last minute I yielded to the persuasion of John R. Mott and went to India with the YMCA to work with students. Pitkin preceded me to the field and landed in China in 1896, financing his own missionary career. On April 27, 1900, he wrote back to Yale from Paotingfu, Shantung Province, that the Boxer mobs intent on killing the "foreign devils and exterminating their religion" had already surrounded them. On June 2 he wrote: "We have no soldiers to trust. It will be but a short time till we know definitely whether we can serve Him better above or here." Shortly afterward a mob stormed the gate of the compound in which Pitkin was endeavoring to defend the women. He was beheaded and his head offered at the shrine of the Boxer god, while his body was thrown outside the city wall in a pit with nine Chinese Christians.

Fourteen years later in that city I spoke daily for two hours to three thousand Chinese students, some of whom had seen those martyrs die. I could find no better illustration of the cross of Christ than Pitkin, who had given his fortune and his life, and in his dying message had asked

31

that his son take up his unfinished work. Pitkin won more men by his death than he ever could have won by his life.

In September, 1896, I landed in India. Toward dawn of our last day on the ship I stood alone in the bow and watched the dark hills rising in the mist. Clouds hung like a pall over the hot tropical land, but as the day broke we seemed to be speeding toward "the shores of light." With a full heart I sang into the wind,

> The morning light is breaking
> The darkness disappears.

That dawn seemed a portent of a new day in which I firmly believed.

The people of India seemed most attractive—intelligent, courteous, lovable; in the South they excelled in the passive virtues, while in the North they adhered to more warlike traditions. They were more deeply religious than the Anglo-Saxons of North America and had a greater affinity for spiritual concerns than the other peoples of the Far East. I had gone out to India admiring her noble past but I found an immediate appeal in her desperate present. Great numbers of the three hundred million people lived in unthinkable poverty on five cents a day. The masses were sunk in illiteracy, idolatry, devil worship. Over two hundred languages and dialects separated them, and their loyalties were further divided betwen eight principal religions. But the castes, of which there were over two thousand, formed the greatest barriers because people could not cross caste lines to intermarry or even to interdine.

During six decades of experience in India I have witnessed great changes. In 1898 I saw Lord Curzon land as one of the last proud autocratic Viceroys; I watched his unpopular partition of Bengal in an attempt to break Indian opposition to British rule. The typical Tory philosophy, then dominant, was expressed by Winston Churchill as late as 1929, "The idea that India is a nation or can ever be fashioned into a nation is known to be a delusion." I saw the rapid rise of the Nationalist Movement accelerated by Asiatic success in the Russo-Japanese war of 1905. I saw Britain respond to the passionate desire of the Indians for self-government by granting three concessions a decade apart; but they proved to be too little and too late to meet India's demands. In 1930 I saw the Indian National Congress adopt almost unanimously a Declaration of Independence and unfurl their national flag. Self-government would only have been achieved in England's promised "fullness of time" (the Indians asked whether this fullness would occur in time or eternity) had it not been for the action of one man—Gandhi. For thirty-three years I followed Gandhi's work, from 1915 when he first came back to India from South Africa until his death in 1948. If one may say it reverently, the goal of Gandhi, like that of Socrates and Jesus, could be achieved only through his death. We will look into Gandhi's significant place in India in a later chapter.

When I landed in India the bubonic plague was raging, taking a toll of two hundred lives a day in the city of Bombay alone. Ignorant of germs and sanitation, the people were hiding their sick and dead, and soldiers were searching every house, every room, and even every suspicious bundle. When I reached Poona, near Bombay, I joined one of these searching parties and thus had an early opportunity to see the home conditions of the people. Among well-to-do families each house had its family shrine, like a tiny temple, with red-painted stones and small brass idols, flower-strewn for daily worship. The dwellings of the poor were mud houses with leaky roofs; crude ladders led to dark attics or holes into which the people crawled at night. The soldiers had already found over a hundred plague cases and some forty corpses hidden away. One of the latter had been placed in a sitting posture among a group of the living.

I saw something of the famine of 1896, and later the greater famine of 1900, which resulted in the death of five million people and left fifty millions hungry. In an area five times that of England the cattle were gone, streams were dry, wells were empty, and the silent people were huddled specters. I visited Pandita Ramabai, one of the great women of the world, who had saved two thousand child widows and orphans in her wonderful orphanage, rescuing these children from the clutches of the traffickers in human flesh. In the early days of this famine I sent home a report letter asking help. Friends in America responded by sending $17,000 for famine relief and the rescue of orphans. Somehow the letter was copied by the press, and money came from American Indians, Negroes, and twelve different nationalities. One girls' school in China sent an offering for Indian famine relief just before the girls themselves were martyred in the Boxer uprising.

Once at work in India I could see the results of the lives of William Carey, Alexander Duff, and the great missionary educators, such as Dr. Miller of Madras, whose "boys" as distinguished graduates were leading almost every reform movement in the land. I began work in India as College Secretary of the Young Men's Christian Association and as Traveling Secretary of the Student Volunteer Movement in India and Ceylon. Although I had received a full theological training I wanted to work as a layman in the broad Christian movements that brought me in contact with men of all religions rather than to be confined to a particular denomination.

Those first days in India were days of great pressure. The extent of the field, the terrific need of the people, the realization that my one life had to count and that a life is short when viewed in the perspective of India's long problems—these were part of the forces that consciously and unconsciously drove me to desperate efforts.

As I read my records I can see that I was terribly in earnest about my work. Soon after arriving on the field a few of us in the spirit of crusaders started an annual day of prayer for the awakening of India. If any task was hard, sacrificial, extreme, or required a faith that could remove mountains it made a deep appeal to me. Some of us thought we were writing a new Acts of the Apostles. We seemed to be witnessing spiritual miracles and answered prayer. We caught the spirit of the land where Gautama Buddha had tried his experiment of extreme asceticism and for which Gandhi had taken the equivalent of the vows of poverty, chastity, and obedience to free India without violence. A multitude of Christian monks and Indian ascetics all about us were living the sacrificial life.

All unconsciously I was on the verge of asceticism and at times even of fanaticism. For a while I lived as a pure vegetarian in order not to offend high-caste Hindus. For a time

I also lived under what we called divine healing, without a doctor or medicines. Since we seemed to be living among spiritual miracles I even took off my glasses and expected a miraculous cure like the blind man of old. I had to learn my bitter lesson the hard way. I finally discovered, as Hudson Taylor had done in China, that "trust in God should never lessen our use of means, and the use of means should not lessen our trust in God." It was not a question of "either-or" but of "both-and." I had to learn that man's first temptation is to the sins of the flesh, to seek to turn the hard stones of reality into the bread of self-satisfaction. His second temptation is to asceticism or fanaticism, to cast himself down from the temple in order to force God to a miracle by his bold faith. I had to learn that "again it is written" not to tempt God.

For many months the lift of high endeavor and the transforming success of the Christian message all but took the place of sleep and food for me. Then the inevitable happened. In the phrase of my boyhood, "all that goes up must come down," and my indomitable high spirits took the first tumble. No doubt my young compatriots and I had staked out too broad a claim. Moreover, we had neither the training nor the patience to sense the deep psychological tensions of the people, and even of the missionary personnel. Some of our most cherished dreams—often the largest, the most daring—banged into reality with a repercussion which made us realize that we had to think in terms of a longer time-span than we had hoped.

In November, 1897, I came to the darkest day of my life. Looking back over my year in India I felt that I had miserably failed. I knew that I was suffering from over-

work, that I was troubled with insomnia and on the verge
of nervous prostration. I had touched bottom for I was dis-
illusioned, discouraged, bitter, rebellious. Far from home,
at Mhow in western India, after an almost sleepless night,
on my face, too exhausted to get up, I cried to God to show
me the way out. I still believed in God, though I had
utterly failed. On a sudden, with all the objectivity of a
spoken word the truth rang out: "Whoever drinks and
keeps drinking of the water of life that I shall give him
shall never thirst again. This water of life (the life of God
in the soul of man shared with his fellow men) shall become like a well, like a spring, like a fountain, leaping up
forever in fresh life within him."

Years before, I had heard Hudson Taylor testify that
this promise of John 4:14 had been literally fulfilled for
twenty years in his life in inland China. To be sure, I had
tried drinking of this living water for a while, immature
as I was and fulfilling no necessary conditions, but I had
soon found, like Jeremiah, that I was drinking from
"broken cisterns that could hold no water." I then thought
that such a satisfying experience was not for me or for
anyone of my temperament, but only for mountain-peak
men like Hudson Taylor. For years my religious experience
had been up and down, elated and then depressed, encouraged and then discouraged, a victim both of outward
circumstances and of inward feelings. Even if I tried again
I would probably fail as before.

Actually the word did not say "whoever drinks once"
but, in the original, "whoever drinks and keeps drinking,"
in the daily inflow and overflow of abundant spiritual life.
The promise was for "whoever" would keep drinking, ful-

filling certain simple conditions. Then I remembered the word written by John Wesley on the flyleaf of his Bible: "Live today!" I cannot explain it but I arose that morning with a new faith. I had been depressed, now I was exultant. I had been defeated, now I knew triumph. I had been exhausted, now I felt power surging through me. And from that moment to this, nearly six decades later, I have never known an hour of darkness or despair or even of discouragement. I mean this literally. Only God knows how many mistakes I have made since then; how many failures, how many faults and sins mar my record. But day in and day out through the years the fountain of living water has continued to surge up from within—so long as I "keep drinking." I now know in the depths of my being that God satisfies.

This may be accounted incredible by those who do not have this same realization. As it has been the most important experience of my life I must make clear that it has not depended upon a past hour of ecstasy in India years ago, but that certain conditons have continually to be fulfilled. In those early years I was much impressed by the habits of the young man of Nazareth. Three times it is written that he did certain things "as his custom was." As his custom was, he went to the synagogue on the Sabbath day and stood up to read the Scriptures. As his custom was, he went out to pray on the Mount of Olives. As his custom was, "he taught them again" in a life of ceaseless service (Luke 4:16, 17; 22:39; Mark 10:1, 44, 45).

I am not concerned here with the strict exegesis of these passages, but for me devotionally they meant three things: first, feeding upon the truth; second, breathing the breath of prayer in constant fellowship with God; and third, spiritual exercise in service for my fellow men. At the Kansas City Student Volunteer Convention I watched Mott and Speer bending over the little diary kept by John Wesley while he was in Georgia in 1736 and 1737. They were avidly noting the morning periods in Wesley's life, beginning daily at four A.M. I thought I could see something of the spiritual power of Wesley in the lives of these two men and I believed that the habits of all three were consciously seeking to follow "in his steps."

Later Robert Speer wrote me: "For nearly sixty years Bible study has been for me the greatest intellectual and spiritual pleasure of life. . . . As to prayer it is 'the Christian's vital breath.' I do not know what one would do without these periods." Mott wrote me : "Personally I owe more to this habit [of the 'morning watch' which Bishop Moule, Bishop of Durham, had urged upon him] than to any other, unless it be the habit of conclusive thinking."

I am still keeping up these three habits. Although I am reading rapidly scores of other books, I am also reading the whole Bible through again, at least a chapter at a sitting, as I have read it before studiously and slowly. I begin every day with prayer, which is now the greatest joy of my life. And I seek to continue in service. One day at a time I simply seek to live by faith, hope, and love, and on these terms all life is a joy. And assuredly the joy is the greater because its roots reach back so many years into those early days in India when my life was being renewed in a faith which needed daily nurture and the support of trustworthy habits of devotion.

On November 10, 1898, I was married to Miss Maud

Arden. Earlier in my missionary career I had jokingly helped to form the "Bachelors' Anti-matrimonial League" and had boasted that I would never be ensnared. But I had reckoned without the lady. Her father, the Reverend A. H. Arden, had been an Anglican missionary in India. On the return voyage after a furlough in England, Maud Arden saw her father collapse at her feet after conducting the Sunday service on the ship and die immediately. Within a few hours after she landed in India I was introduced to her in the home of a friend in Madras. I capitulated on the spot but her response was less rapid and she kept me in agonized suspense for an eternity—well, a full month!

Maud was peculiarly fitted to the life she shared with me. She had a natural goodness found more often, perhaps, among unintellectual persons. But she was an intellectual. She had the quiet patience of a woman who lives serenely among the same neighbors all of her days. But she lived all over the globe. She had curiously, surely one of God's best gifts to man and one which must be constantly exercised and satisfied if it is to remain acute. She had a kind of fourth-dimensional awareness, a sensitivity to life in all its outreach. And she had a sense of humor—which means that she kept her perspective. A noted psychic said of her that she had the most beautiful aura, the nearest to the true white of the saints, that he had ever seen. People felt this quality in her and I never knew a group or even a person who did not make her welcome.

After working a little more than a year among Indian college students, holding meetings during the day and lecturing to Hindu students at night, I gradually came to the realization that the time had not yet come to reap among these proud peoples. I discovered that no missionary in India at that time, whether educator or evangelist, was averaging one baptized convert a year among the high-caste Hindu or Mohammedan students. Therefore I shifted my major work from the colleges to the Indian churches, although I kept my connection with the YMCA. I felt at that time that if the Indian church was thoroughly aroused, then the Indians themselves would in time win the higher as well as the lower castes, and that India would be converted to Christianity as surely as had been the Roman Empire.

Of course, in order to work in the churches it was necessary that I learn a native language. I chose the Tamil language because, although it was the most difficult in the country, it gave me access to the largest number of Christians in the older and more advanced missions. While I was concentrating on language study one of the missionaries in our group broke down and my wife and I were asked to occupy his station at Batlagundu in the Madura mission of the American Board (Congregationalist). Then another missionary became ill and was ordered home and I was asked to take over his theological seminary. I agreed to this assignment if I could put the seminary on wheels and take the men out to preach among the masses for a year. My wife helped to run the mission station while I was traveling, and because we were located miles from a railway station or doctor, every morning she had a score of patients on the veranda, suffering from every complaint, including the deadly cholera. Their trust in her and their love for her was one of the beautiful experiences of my life.

Our seminary-on-wheels worked out a schedule that

used every minute of the day to the greatest advantage. Each morning at four or five o'clock our little American alarm clock would sputter in the darkness, and immediately from the score of workers in the adjoining tent there rose the sound of a Tamil lyric. After our "morning watch" by candlelight, and a cup of coffee, we were off in half a dozen parties of three or four men each to visit the villages within a four-mile radius. Entering a village we would strike up with a violin and a Tamil song; the crowd would gather, and we would speak in the street and interview the people personally. After a long morning's work, exhausted by the tropical sun and visits to several villages, we would return to camp for the midday meal and a nap before the study hour and the daily theological class in the tent. In the late afternoon we visited the nearer villages, and at night some neighboring town where hundreds would eagerly follow the magic-lantern story of the life of Christ.

As we walked through the fields each day I would take a mile or two alone with each man. We would first take up the problems of his own life. Then I would assign him a text or theme and give him time to prepare an outline for a sermon or address, which we would then discuss. About the finest compliment I ever received was to overhear a student one day comment in the vernacular, "He is a native. He is one of us except in color."

During the year, by reaching some 20 villages a day, from 57 encampments, we visited 116 congregations and 1,937 Hindu villages; we gave medical treatment to over 6,000 patients who were far from any hospital and spoke to over 130,000 hearers.

During the early years in India I suffered greatly at

times from insomnia and overwork. Finally the doctor said that I must find a hobby or I would be a "dead duck." When he asked if I would not enjoy stamp or coin collecting I told him either one would bore me to death or drive me to drink. Trite but none the less true. When he asked what I liked best to do I told him that as a boy I had always been fond of shooting. "There's your hobby," he said. "Get a rifle and forget your troubles out in the elephant and tiger jungle." And that was just what I did. In a barren portion of my mission station in the Madura district of South India there were hundreds of wild elephant; and in the dust of the road as we entered the jungle there were more footprints of tiger than of man. Also, in the hills near Kodaikanal, where some of the missionaries spent a portion of the hot season, game was abundant.

So whenever I realized that I had been working too strenuously for common sense I took to the hills with a new rifle, a .405 five-shot Winchester, and Sampson, a native hunter. Each night of our first hunt we slept in a great cave. The first morning, as Sampson swept the horizon with my field glasses, he sighted a herd of mountain ibex— like our bighorn of the West. We crossed the valley and climbed the next mountain. Just as I peeked over the cliff a young ibex paused a split second to see what we might be—and my first shot furnished us with fresh meat, which we had from then on.

The next morning we sighted a herd of Indian bison, not like our dull slow-moving American buffalo, but swift, deadly, and hard to kill. All day we climbed, over a mountain and across a valley until we came within sight of the herd. This was my first shot at big game, and I was not an expert with the rifle. I recalled the grave in our little churchyard near my home in the Kodai hills where a man lay buried who had been horned by a wounded bison. On his tombstone were the words "Beside the still waters." I did not wish a similar memorial. Sampson and I withdrew for a council of war. We decided that I should take off my heavy shoes so as to stalk the herd noiselessly. We also agreed that when we came upon the bison I would shoot three times and then if the bison who was my target was only wounded we would run to the nearest cliff; I would leap to the right-hand branch of the tree overhanging the cliff and he would jump to the left branch beyond reach of the bison's horns if he charged us. We then approached the herd and I was about to shoot when Sampson whispered: "We could never make that cliff with a wounded bison charging us. Stand on my back, climb up into this tree and shoot from the lower branches—and hit your mark." Just as I reached my position in the tree the bison saw me and sprang up. I fired, broke its back on the first shot, then killed it with the second. As sunset was already approaching we left the carcass and climbed far into the night to reach our cave. When we returned the next day to get the horns and head we found that two tigers had dragged the carcass for more than a mile and had fed upon the hind quarters. But we brought in our trophy!

The third day we followed the footprints of a tiger but never got in sight of it for a shot. On the fourth morning we sighted an elk, or *sambar*, but I could see no horns and refused to break the law by shooting a female. The poor coolie who was following us to get meat begged me to shoot it, saying that it would keep his family supplied with dried meat for the entire winter. I told him I would surely try to get him his meat before night. Shortly after that I saw Sampson running down from the hills. "Bear, big black bear!" he called. We ran up the hill so fast that when we came in sight of the bear I was breathless, so that on the first shot I only wounded the huge fellow in the hip. He roared and started down the mountain full speed. My second shot was aimed more carefully and broke his back so that he rolled some fifty feet down the mountainside. The third shot I tried to make fatal by aiming at his neck.

We pushed forward through the deep grass, breast high. It was nervous work; I did not know whether at any moment the wounded bear would rise to claw me, but suddenly we came upon him stone dead. During the night Sampson and the coolie spent hours skinning the bear and bringing in the meat, so that they each had a supply of curried bear's meat for the winter and I had the skin for a handsome rug. In four days of shooting in the hills I had bagged an ibex, a bison, and a bear; but that kind of game was tame compared to the elephants and tigers waiting on the jungle plains below.

Ambitious for a huge tusk for a trophy we spent several days hunting wild elephant. Coming home very weary one night we saw ahead of us in the broad path of the moonlight what appeared to be two great oak trees. But as we approached they walked off and we discovered we were in the middle of a herd of wild elephants! The jungle was far too dense for us to try to get around the herd. I remembered that there were two points at which you can pierce the brain of an elephant but I also knew that even under favorable conditions in the daylight such a shot required cool and exact aiming. I wished that we were perched in a *howdah* on the back of a tame elephant, as the guests of some Indian princes go shooting in deluxe style! I wondered what my Indian companion would do and was amazed to watch him walk swiftly into the midst of the herd, making the squeak of the little field mouse of which all elephants are deathly afraid. I suppose their fear is based on the fact that the inside of their sensitive trunks is vulnerable to the little animal. Whatever the reason, the herd separated and retreated into the jungle and we walked quickly through, like the Israelites on dry land in the midst of the Red Sea.

Another evening during a time of drought we reached a water hole far out in the jungle. From miles around game would have to come in to drink at night and if we were seated high in the branches of a great tree above the hole we would be able to see to shoot by the light of full moon. But just at sunset we heard the dreadful muffled roar of the *verum puli*, or empty tiger, hunting for his prey. When this animal has been long without meat and his stealth has yielded no kill, he roars fiercely and then listens as the frightened deer and other game break away noisily through the brush. Then he follows the sound till he picks up the scent, steals up, and springs upon his prey. Since the tiger could pick us out of the tree with one spring, our only safety was to get out of the jungle. But we could not get out that night. So our native guide built a roaring fire which no tiger would dare approach, kept it going all night as he sat with his rifle across his knees, while we rolled up in our blankets and slept on dry ground out in the open.

We got no game that night, but I found there was more excitement in being game than in bagging game.

One day when we started out for wild elephant we sighted a herd of bison. I suggested that we shoot one and leave the carcass as bait for a tiger. So we shot the bison and as we followed the wounded animal a young bull bison calf that had been asleep in the grass sprang up and tried to escape. We surrounded and captured him, brought him back to camp and soon had him tamed, feeding him on condensed milk from a sponge. We called him "Billy" for Buffalo Bill. I knew of no bison like him in captivity.

On one occasion I went out for elephants with a retired English major. To get a shot at the tusker, which is often in the center of the herd, you have to creep into the midst of the elephants on foot while their great trunks are above you feeding on the high branches of the trees. The great danger is that the cows may catch your scent and charge you in order to defend their young. No hundred-yard Olympic champion can outrun a wild elephant, and when you are in the middle of a herd you always remember that you are no champion at any distance.

On this occasion I was nervous but I tried to remember William James' admonition, which in substance was: "Act brave and you will feel brave." I spat like a Bowery tough and started for the herd. As we approached the huge animals I noted the color of the major's face—a ghastly yellow-blue. Evidently he was afraid and I knew that I was. I will have to confess that on a former occasion following a tusker I had bolted, run a few yards, and missed my shot.

When a hunter is about to approach a herd of elephants on foot it is the custom for him to scoop up a handful of dust and drop it to see if there is any drift in the air; then he can keep away from the windward side of the herd. In spite of these precautions, the major and I must have got too far to windward. After we had spent an hour trying to penetrate the herd, suddenly the whole herd set up a dreadful trumpeting as from a hundred trumpeters. Joshua's ram's-horns would never have been heard in this noise! The sound struck terror to my very soul and this time there was no time to spit or act brave. Would they charge us or run the other way? I saw the leader lift his trunk and catch our scent. I aimed swiftly for the one spot in the forehead where the brain could be pierced, and fired. The huge bulk fell with a crash. Shooting an elephant in India was as simple as shooting a rabbit in Kansas.

As the years went by nothing was so exciting or so energy-renewing for me as shooting in the jungle. However, I never became a big-game hunter. The object of these expeditions was not to gain trophies but health, and that I found for both body and mind. I always returned with fresh vigor and better perspective to the work which I was trying to carry on.

Our mission station at Batlagundu in the Madura district was responsible for fifty square miles on the denominational checkerboard of India. We were located miles from any railway far down in the tropics just ten degrees above the equator. The climate was said to be "three months hot and nine months hotter," so we slept in a mat shed on the roof in order to get every possible breath of air. Our mission staff consisted of one elderly missionary who worked in the hills, myself, and about a hundred

Indian fellow workers scattered throughout the district. Most of these men taught a village school six days a week and then conducted Sunday services among a population of 5,000 Christians and some 500,000 Hindus and Mohammedans. When on tour I traveled in a two-wheeled bullock cart at two miles an hour until the laymen of Denver gave me a motorcycle—at the same time that they gave Samuel Zwemer a fast camel for the sands of Arabia.

Our mission compound was the proverbial beehive of activity. In the center stood the little church teaching a new way of life for India under the direction of the golden-hearted Indian pastor who assisted in the care of the whole station. When I say "assisted" I use the word in the Western sense, which means that he actually did most of the work but was not adequately paid for it. Here also was our boarding school for a hundred students whom we were trying to train to be India's future leaders, for always we sought to develop indigenous rather than foreign leadership.

After acquiring the Tamil language I spent half my time using the vernacular throughout South India while the other and more important half was devoted to a broader field of service which took me all over India with my fellow worker, Azariah. Our first object was the awakening and deepening of the spiritual life of the pastors, catechists, teachers, and laymen of the Christian churches for their own work in the evangelization of all India. Each year at the invitation of the missionaries we visited some sixty centers, an average of more than one a week, in some twenty missions. Yearly we conducted more than a score of conferences for Christian workers in Tamil with the attendance ranging from twenty-five to five hundred, and in each community we held meetings in the Tamil churches in the evenings. We also conducted lectures in English in a score of college centers and cities with an attendance ranging from fifty to three hundred. Like John Wesley we sought to develop small, intimate, and vital groups of men. In addition we wrote and printed books in English and Tamil, selling at cost about 20,000 a year. A decade or more later E. Stanley Jones took up this traveling work, speaking and writing in English; still later came his ashrams, which have had such a deep spiritual influence in both India and America.

The deepest satisfaction of my years in India was watching the powerful leadership which many of the Indian Christians developed. Indeed, the supreme adventure of my life has been not in seeking to do a great work myself but in searching for men who could do "greater works" than I could. In public meetings and in personal contacts my aim has been to challenge the conscience and move the will; to call men to decision about their way of life and to urge them to immediate action.

If in India my efforts for an entire year could not win a single convert from among the Brahmans or Moslems I still believed that somewhere there were indigenous leaders who could win all of India, high caste and low caste. My calling was to find these men. I sought them in every interview and in every audience. When I found a possible leader we developed a close friendship. These men were friends with whom I could be frank and sincere and with whom I could share the best that I had. Among the greatest souls I would mention five: K. T. Paul, Francis

Kingsbury, Pastor Santiago, Bishop Azariah, and Bishop Abraham.

K. T. Paul has well been called the John R. Mott of India. He was a man capable of deep and lasting friendship, of good counsel, and of wise decisions. He had already studied law, held a government position, and been headmaster of the Arcot Mission High School at Punganur when he came in 1903 to teach in the Madras Christian College. It was here one night, standing in the moonlight and looking into the depths of his heart, that I placed my hand on his shoulder and challenged him to give his whole life to the newly organized National Missionary Society even though this work offered him no financial security.

"K. T.," as he was affectionately called by his friends, had been one of the seventeen Indian delegates, representing the provinces of India, Burma, and Ceylon, who had met in the historic library of William Carey at Serampore on Christmas Day, 1905, and organized the National Missionary Society. The purpose of the Society was to enable the Indian Christians of all Protestant churches to work in the neediest provinces for the evangelization of their own country. The constitution of the Society was adopted in the pagoda where Henry Martin had worked a century earlier. "K. T." devoted himself to the work of the Society until 1912, when he became the YMCA's Associate National Secretary for India; four years later he was elevated to the responsible position of national general secretary. He gave twenty-five years of service to these organizations. The strain and stress of the crusade for India's freedom carried him to an untimely grave at the age of fifty-four. Through the years I have had a close working relationship with many of Asia's great Christians, but of them all I consider K. T. Paul the wisest.

Another dear Indian friend and fellow worker was Francis Kingsbury. His father, a great Hindu scholar, was the leading opponent of Christianity. As a boy, Francis was deeply religious and was trained in his Hindu sacred books. Imbibing his father's prejudice, he so resented Christ and Christianity that he had drawn a picture of Christ on the cross, in effigy, that he might kick it every day of his life, and thus relieve his feelings of hatred. But later as he read the story of Jesus, his heart was melted and he finally yielded his life to Christ. He became a Christian worker, and I rejoiced at his great power with large audiences of turbulent Hindu students.

Next was my beloved Pastor Santiago. As a boy he was an untouchable pariah; the dogs might enter a Brahman street but not he; the sacred cow was welcome in the Hindu temple, but there was no room for the polluted outcaste, dwelling apart in filth and ignorance and superstition. An elderly American friend of mine contributed twenty dollars a year to make it possible for this handicapped boy to go to a mission high school, and then he was helped to work his way through college. After teaching in the theological seminary, he became our pastor at Batlagundu, South India, where we shared many joyous years. When his services were needed as mayor of the town, Hindus and Mohammedans joined in a written petition to the government that the former pariah, Santiago, be appointed. When the United Church of South India was formed, Santiago was chosen as its able moderator. It was a joy to work with this glorious character, sunny, attractive, lovable; an earnest evangelist, a spiritual pastor, and a wise leader of the Indian church.

The greatest man whose life I was ever privileged to share was V. S. Azariah. With Azariah I visited his home out in the heart of the Tinnevelly district, South India, near the village of Megnanapuram, "The Town of True Wisdom." High over the palm trees I saw the spire of its great stone church, which seats three thousand. Formerly on this very spot had stood the devil temple, the center of worship for his people, the Shanars, a tree-climbing caste, declared outcastes by the law courts, forbidden to enter the Hindu temples. At the entrance to the church I saw the altar stone which once had reeked with the blood of beasts sacrificed to the devils in the old temple. When the last devil-worshiper had been converted to Christianity, with their own hands the people had torn down their devil temple and erected in its place this great stone church.

Azariah was not brilliant, but he was fearlessly honest, faithful and hard-working, with a winsome and attractive personality. He always carried some book, never wasting a moment. I watched him grow, first as a student, then as a young secretary of the YMCA, then as a traveling fellow evangelist using Tamil and English in our work in India, Burma, and Ceylon, finally as the greatest bishop I knew in all Asia.

One night in 1902, when we were working together in Jaffna, North Ceylon, he went out under the palm trees and shed bitter tears because he saw the Jaffna Foreign Missionary Society sending its Tamil missionaries to India, while the 60,000 Christians in his own mission were doing so little for the evangelization of their own country. When he returned to India he gathered together the young men of the churches and on February 12, 1903, they organized the Indian Missionary Society of Tinnevelly and sent their first workers to the Telugu country in the state of Hyderabad. When the National Missionary Society was organized in 1905 Azariah became its secretary. Working for both of these indigenous societies Azariah went across the country organizing a new missionary crusade, calling on students to go as missionaries to their own people and urging the churches to give in sacrificial service for their own country.

Then in 1909 Azariah felt called to give up this most useful work to go out himself as a missionary among the neediest of his own people. He chose for his field the most degraded, drunken, carrion-eating devil-worshipers in Hyderabad. The poverty of the people, struggling to live on four or five cents a day, was abysmal. In fact, the people were so degraded that I did not expect to see any appreciable results in our lifetime. I pleaded with Azariah not to throw away his life there, and I said good-by fearing I should never see him again.

But three years later I saw him consecrated as the first Indian Anglican bishop—consecrated by a group of English bishops from Oxford and Cambridge with a thousand years of Christian civilization and culture behind them, while behind Azariah was the abyss of the past, a thousand years of the devil worship of outcastes. He became the Bishop of Dornakal, and probably the strongest and most effective bishop in India or in all Asia.

When I made my last visit to Dornakal in 1949, I found that it had become the largest mission station on earth and perhaps the most deeply spiritual work in the whole mission field. Azariah served as bishop from 1912 to 1946, for thirty-four years, leaving a Christian community which today numbers over 400,000—more converts than in the whole of Japan. Whole communities had now been lifted above their former debased life. Most of the new converts, with an attendance of some seventy thousand in their scattered churches, gathered every night in the week for the study of the New Testament in order to conform their lives to the way of Christ. So great had been the moral transformation of these low-caste people that over ten thousand from the higher and middle castes within the diocese, convinced of the moral superiority of the Christian way of life, had also joined the church.

Among the converts in Dornakal I met Lakshikadu, a former robber, who described to me his technique of robbery. But when he became a Christian and heard that Jesus had worked as a carpenter, he eagerly learned that trade, working six days a week to support his family and on the seventh day going out to tell the Good News to his former fellow robbers and to the outcastes. He worked without a salary and had already won two small congregations of new converts.

At the other end of the social scale were two Brahman converts, who worked under Bishop Azariah receiving no salary, only their food and clothing.

I had once bought a little land for Azariah's industrial school for fifty cents an acre and for some years had contributed to the school's support, but finally dropped the practice. Then one day, about 1920, without knowing why, I suddenly felt called upon to scrape together all I could and to send him a thousand dollars. Later I learned that this gift was the instrument used to answer prayer. When I sent the money I had no definite cause in mind, for details of his situation had escaped my mind. I had quite forgotten that the Methodists had work in the same community in which the Anglicans were established, making two competing denominations in a field which could be more effectively served by one united church. I did not know that the Hyderabad Annual Methodist Conference had recently decided to concentrate their efforts elsewhere and had offered to leave the whole field to Bishop Azariah's Anglicans under Indian leadership, turning over all their property—residence, churches, and schools—if the debt upon them could be paid. This transaction involved a few thousand dollars, with the immediate need of one thousand dollars in cash. Azariah had said to his wife, "We will pray about this tonight, and tomorrow I'll write to Sherwood Eddy and ask him if he can secure the money for us. We've been working for one united church for this area ever since the Edinburgh Conference in 1910 and we must not miss this opportunity." In the morning, before he could write his letter, my letter arrived containing a draft for a thousand dollars. Answered prayer was one of the continuing realities of our fifteen years in India.

In 1910 Azariah and I had gone as delegates to the World Missionary Conference at Edinburgh. At that time we did not see how the feeble forces of existing missions, divided between a hundred competing sects, could ever win India, but the two of us "agreed" in the terms of Matthew 18:19 to pray in faith for the union of our divided churches, and we continued to pray for thirty-

five years, while Azariah himself led in the work for this
union until his death on January 2, 1945. Two years later,
delegates met in the great cathedral in Madras to form
the Church of South India, with over a million members,
uniting the Episcopal Anglicans, the Methodists, Pres-
byterians, and Congregational churches in one organic
union. It is the only place I know on earth where Episcopal
and nonepiscopal churches have combined in one organic
union since they were divided four centuries ago by the
Reformation.

Another beloved bishop in India was Bishop Abraham,
the Reformed Syrian Bishop in Travancore. Abraham was
just a lad when first I saw him in a meeting with a score
of boys from the Syrian Church. I fear I was blunt and
tactless when I spoke to those Syrian lads from Travancore, as I said: "Boys, you claim that your church was
founded here in India by the Apostle Thomas nineteen
centuries ago. Whether it was or not, your church has been
spiritually asleep for a thousand years. The impoverished
masses in your country are sunk in idolatry, superstition,
and ignorance. Many of you are cramming to get your
degrees, to rush out into life and make money while you
leave your church and country in bitter need. Will none of
you dare to take up the cross of Christ and follow him for
the awakening of the Syrian Church and the evangelization of your own country?"

The meeting apparently ended in failure. But years
afterward Abraham told me that out under the stars that
night he paced up and down and could not sleep. As he
wrestled with himself, he said: "It is true. Our church is
asleep, our country is in desperate need, while I am going

out to make money and live for my own selfish ambition."
He told me that for days, for weeks, he fought his battle,
until finally he yielded his entire life for the service of his
own people.

In 1912 Abraham began his theological education in
Wycliffe College, Toronto. One night he crossed the Canadian border and came to Buffalo to attend a conference
with a group of Canadian students. The Canadians registered at an American hotel, but as soon as Abraham's
darker face appeared the clerk said the hotel was "full."
In protest, the Canadian students left in a body and went
to another hotel, where the Indian was received. But
Abraham could not sleep. He was humiliated and lacer-
ated in spirit by the indignity. Then he remembered the
outcastes of India who had long been excluded by his
proud, prosperous, and respectable Syrian Church. He had
never supposed they cared about their exclusion, but now
he knew that if they were men of like passions with himself
they suffered from indignities just as he did. Instead of
becoming embittered against Americans for their race
prejudice, he resolved to return to India and to give his
life for the awakening of the people of his ancient church,
that they might receive the outcastes, end the practice of
segregation, and throw themselves into a missionary crusade for the evangelization of India.

In 1918, back in India with his theological degree,
Abraham was consecrated bishop of the Mar Thoma
Syrian Church. One day he asked me to speak to his
people. Annually the Syrian Christians gathered in a con-
vention like the Feast of Tabernacles among the Hebrews.
Erecting a simple palm-leaf pavilion to shut out the sun,

and sitting in the clean white sand of a river bed which is empty during the dry season, some thirty to forty thousand of them gathered in an annual convention in what was perhaps the largest Christian audience in the world. I saw Bishop Abraham welcoming the once-excluded outcastes for baptism, the converts finally totaling over 15,000.

On my last visit to India in 1949 I again spoke to forty thousand Syrian Christians in a great convention. This ancient church, awakened after a thousand years, had become the most zealous church in all India and was now taking a leading part in the evangelization of the country. Yet that first meeting, when I spoke to Abraham and a score of indifferent young Christians, had seemed at the time to be the greatest failure of any meeting in my life.

It was because of Christians like K. T. Paul, Francis Kingsbury, Santiago, Azariah, and Abraham that those of us on the mission field were encouraged to continue our search for indigenous leaders throughout the whole of Asia.

Chapter 3

❧

ASIA IN FERMENT

Among the revolutionary trends that I have witnessed in Asia during the past half-century I rank high the surge of student interest in Christianity. In 1907 I attended the Tokyo conference of the World Student Federation. While there I addressed meetings of Japanese and Chinese students, and then on my return voyage to India I stopped at Hong Kong and held my first meetings there. Ever since that time I have been closely in touch with momentous happenings in Japan, China, Korea, and the Philippines.

The Chinese students whom I met in Tokyo in 1907 had been drawn there by the rise of Japan as a world power. Since the Japanese victory over Russia in 1905, fifteen thousand young Chinese had come to Japan. That victory had sent a thrill over all Asia; an Oriental nation for the first time in modern history had won a war, not only from a European power, but from the giant Russia, hitherto considered invincible.

In China at this time the ancient order was rapidly dying and a new era was being born. The gestation period was rugged indeed. Only twelve years previously China had been humiliated by a crushing defeat in a war with

Japan. By 1907 the great powers had become more aggressive and the partition of China seemed imminent. Graft and corruption were eating the heart out of orderly government. The Chinese people were then the most conservative on earth, still wearing the antiquated queue, long-time symbol of submission to their Manchu conquerors and to a decadent civilization. Foot-binding of girls still prevailed. Ancestor worship laid the heavy hand of the past upon the people.

A century had passed since Robert Morrison, the first modern Protestant missionary, had begun his work at Canton. Morrison had been able to tell the Christian message to only a few trusted Chinese and then behind locked doors—lest they all be arrested. After seven long years he had baptized his first convert, far "away from human observation." In their first twenty-five years Protestant pioneer missionaries baptized only ten Chinese converts, and these in the face of bitter opposition. Even by 1900, when this number had increased to 113,000, the literati remained practically untouched.

The first American secretaries of the YMCA arrived in Japan in 1888, and in China in 1895. In 1898 Fletcher Brockman, with his frail but courageous young wife and their baby, was dumped upon a muddy flat on the river bank near Nanking, at midnight, interdicted from a city surrounded by the greatest city wall in the world, more than twenty miles in circumference and centuries old. China did not want a single element of Brockman's Western civilization—its railways, newspapers, modern science, education, and least of all its religion. As general secretary of the Young Men's Christian Association in China, when Brockman witnessed the stampede of Chinese students to Japan he persuaded the brilliant C. T. Wang, who later became Foreign Minister of the Republic and vice-president of the Senate, to go to Tokyo and open YMCA work among these thousands of homeless students living amid the fierce temptation of a strange city.

Thus, in ways then unknown to me, the stage had been set for the beginning of my forty years of evangelism among Chinese students. In these Tokyo meetings which John R. Mott and I conducted many Chinese students were moved by deep conviction. Some of them became Christians, and large numbers joined Christian Bible classes as honest inquirers. It was then that Brockman, and he alone, saw in this little microcosm of students from all the provinces of China the sudden change of attitude toward Western ideas that was destined soon to spread over the whole of China. He then asked, "Why should we not do in their own land what is being done among these Chinese students in Japan?"

Not long afterward, while we were walking down the streets of Shanghai, he asked if I would come back from India in the near future to give three months to evangelistic meetings among the students of China, saying, "We will guarantee you an audience of a thousand students a night in fifteen cities, with men pledging to accept the Christian life every night if you give them the opportunity to do so." I looked at Brockman askance and wondered whether the tropical sun had affected his brain, or whether this was indeed a vision of faith.

On my way back to India I had been asked to speak at St. Stephen's College in Hong Kong. I would test the possibilities of student interest there, and if I found conditions as Brockman believed them to be, I would return to China as soon as possible for such a campaign as he envisioned. At St. Stephen's College I said to Canon Barnett: "It is a simple matter to speak to your students, but will you let me call for immediate decisions based on the Christian teaching which this college has been giving to these students for years?" He hesitated, for many of his students were from leading families, sons of Confucian officials and Chinese millionaires. It might break up the college if a group of these students abandoned Confucianism and embraced Christianity, for the college had never had a convert. Finally he said, "You may do as you feel led." I saw that he was afraid and I knew that there was good reason for his fear. But we had to make the test.

I spoke to the students for an hour. I reminded them of the then recent Boxer uprising, when some thirty thousand Chinese Christians had lost their lives. I told them that if they embraced this same faith they might be disinherited, deprived of their homes or even of life itself. At the close of the address I asked if there were any who, informed by their long study of Christianity in college, were ready to accept Christ and his way of life, and if so would they rise before the entire college to confess their faith. I made the test as difficult as I could. There was a long embarrassing pause. We had failed.

And then! After forty-seven years I can still see in my mind's eye that first student as he rose, clad in his blue silk robe, still wearing his long queue. He was the leading athlete of the college. Before the entire student body he came forth as the first man in that institution ever to take a stand publicly for Christ and break openly with the old Confucian order. His rising was like an electric shock to the entire student body. One of the most brilliant young students rose next, then the son of a prominent official. Finally nine or ten students were publicly taking their stand for Christ and his revolutionary way of life. The break had come at last, and we believed by that token that we should see "greater works than these" in other cities throughout China.

When I went out to the mission field nearly sixty years ago, there were three Gibraltar rocks that seemed to stand impregnable against the missionary crusade: the Moslem peoples, the Brahmans and higher castes of India, the literati and students of China. Now in the face of this public declaration we joyously believed that the third stronghold was vulnerable and, like the walls of Jericho, about to fall. As a result of this first meeting at Hong Kong I interrupted my work in India in 1908 long enough to share in a stirring series of evangelistic meetings in a dozen cities throughout China.

Everywhere in Asia, during the next few years, Asian students were wakening. During the winter of 1912 and 1913, Dr. John R. Mott and I concentrated on students in a series of evangelistic meetings held throughout Asia. On the opening night in Colombo, Ceylon, we were faced by an audience of eight hundred Ceylonese students, composed of Hindus, Buddhists, Mohammedans, and Christians, both Catholic and Protestant. They had been admitted by ticket and many others had been turned away from the door. One hundred and fifty student Christian workers were stationed throughout the hall to confer with inquirers and conduct follow-up work after the meetings. That first night Dr. Mott plunged straight into his subject, "Sin"; I followed the next night on "Christ"; and by the third night more than two hundred seekers had given their names, promising to read the Gospels and investigate Christianity. These men rose publicly as inquirers, and some seventy-five others confessed Christ—many of them Hindu or Buddhist students, while the others were nominal Christians, largely from the old Portuguese and Dutch missions.

Crossing to India we came to Madras, which proved to be a terrible battlefield with the forces of darkness. Never can I forget the sight of that audience of two thousand non-Christian students, the pick of the Hindu government colleges of the city, crowded into the great Parsee Theater, filling every seat, standing in the aisles, with some hundreds who could not gain admission turned away. The roar of a lion in an adjacent tent added to the difficulties of poor acoustics in the theater; yet night after night, in spite of the warning of Hindu papers against the meetings and in spite of appalling weather, two thousand young Hindus came out through the rain and mud and sat there listening hour after hour to the straightest preaching. Entrenched as they were in centuries of caste, their minds darkened by the mists of pantheism, polytheism, and idolatry, these Hindu students formed one of the hardest audiences we ever faced in Asia.

In Calcutta examinations were on, and some of the colleges were closing for vacation. Yet on the opening night eighteen hundred students crowded the Curzon Theater. The subjects dealt with on five succeeding nights were: "Personal Purity," "The Results of Sin," "Moral Heroism," "Christ the Only Saviour," and "Religion a Matter of the Will."

From India Dr. Mott and I went to China for a memorable tour. We landed three days late because of a storm at sea. He began at Canton, while I conducted meetings in near-by Hong Kong. In spite of midyear vacation and the China New Year's festivities, some fifteen hundred students crowded the large Chinese theater each night. By this time China had become a Republic and the queues were gone forever; socially and politically the conservatism of four thousand years was being cast away. It was in Foochow that the high peak of our evangelism was reached. From there I wrote:

We are just leaving Foochow where we have been working for a week, while Dr. Mott is in Manchuria. Never have I known such an eventful week. While the student audiences averaged a thousand a night in India, and two thousand in other parts of China, here in Foochow five thousand a day, admitted by ticket only, have been attending the meetings, and the total attendance during the six days was over 30,000. The Provincial Parliament itself adjourned and invited Robertson [1] and myself to address them. The leaders of the Chamber of Commerce attended one lecture and a banquet. The Confucian presidents of the thirteen government colleges who had extended the invitation to visit the city postponed the government examinations for a week and closed their colleges during the afternoons that the students might attend. During our stay they invited Professor Robertson and myself to a dinner to discuss plans for helping the students develop their moral character. On the third day we

[1] C. H. Robertson, the brilliant scientist, professor of mechanical engineering, and star athlete of Purdue University, went out to China in 1902. As a unique scientific genius, he lectured for thirty years all over China to tens of thousands of students and officials, as well as in Japan, the Philippines, Siberia, and Russia.

had to conduct an overflow meeting. There was at all times the most rapt attention, and when we called for inquirers over a thousand men promised to join Bible classes to study the four Gospels with open minds, to follow Christ according to their consciences and accept him if they found him true.

As I look back over four decades I can see that we reached high tide in the China campaign of 1914. When we arrived at the Guild Hall in Tientsin, our first city, we found two thousand students crowding every seat, with many turned away. During the week I also addressed meetings of some fifteen hundred younger boys, among whom was the future Confucian statesman Chen Li-fu and many other future leaders. A special meeting for businessmen and gentry was attended by eighteen hundred leading citizens.

The next week we conducted meetings in the old conservative capital of Peking, from which I made this report:

President Yuan Shih-kai received us and expressed deep interest in the meetings. He is liberally contributing every year to our Association work. The Vice-president of the Republic, General Li Yuan Hung, whom I had known last year as Governor at Wuchang, gave us a special luncheon and requested us to address his family and guests on the subject of Christianity. The Ministry of the Interior at their own suggestion granted us a site for a pavilion for the evangelistic meetings within the Forbidden City itself, opposite the palace of the Dowager Empress who put Christians to death fourteen years ago.

It is the first time in history that Christian meetings have been allowed within this sacred precinct. Strangely enough, the Ministry suggested that we place this pavilion next to the sacred altar where the emperor annually worshipped the Spirit of the Land. The Ministry of War granted two hundred tents from the army to make the pavilion rainproof. The Minister of Education granted a half-holiday to all government students in Peking to enable them to attend the opening meeting, while the Minister of Foreign Affairs sent his representative to the meeting. On the third night we spoke for over an hour on "Jesus Christ, the Hope of China." More than a thousand men signed cards as inquirers to join Bible classes.

In Changsha, in far Hunan, the seat of the Yale-in-China Mission, I had a marvelous experience when I spoke to audiences of three thousand students a day, with a thousand Confucian students desiring to enter Bible classes as inquirers. This was the capital of a province that was long the most bigoted in China. I remember writing a little pamphlet sixty years ago, *The Supreme Decision of the Christian Student*, appealing for volunteers to enter this unoccupied province of Hunan, with a population of more than twenty millions of people, without a single missionary or Christian worker. It was Frank Keller of our class at Yale who as a medical missionary had had the honor of opening up this province at the risk of his life and who was waiting to receive us as we entered the city. As we left the steamer and entered the great gates of the ancient walled city we saw posters announcing the evangelistic meetings on the very notice boards where a few years earlier had hung the edict to kill the "foreign devils" who had come to make medicine out of the eyes of kidnaped children!

The changed attitude was personified in our interpreter, C. L. Nieh, who stood out as a striking object-lesson before the students and the whole province. He was a member of a leading family; his father had been governor of four provinces; his uncle, Marquis Tseng, was successively

China's Minister to England, France, Germany, and Russia ; his grandfather, Tseng Kuo-fan, was China's greatest statesman of the century. Nieh had been a young Confucian atheist when taken for a spy while with the Red Cross at the front in the civil war of 1913 and had been arrested and thrown into prison at Wuchang. There he had a decisive religious experience and upon his release was baptized a Christian. I could write of a hundred great interpreters like this man, with whom I had the privilege of working during six decades.

We had another glorious experience in Hangchow, the classical city famous in the annals of Marco Polo. The Civil Governor granted a half-holiday to the students on three successive days so that they could attend the meetings, and on the second day his personal representative took the chair. After we had spoken for an hour on "Jesus Christ," an opportunity was given for those who wished to join Bible classes to do so. More than a thousand students enrolled themselves as inquirers. Our interpreter at these meetings was C. T. Wang, then the brilliant Christian statesman, formerly a member of Yuan's cabinet and vice-president of the national Senate.

On the second night the Military Governor, the Civil Governor, and the officials of the province invited Wang and me to a banquet. After dinner the Governor requested us to address them. Seated next to the Civil Governor was his young Secretary of State, Mr. S. T. Wen, who I felt was not far from the Kingdom of God. After I had stated the claims of Christianity, while the interpreter was talking with the Governor about personal religion, I went over to the Secretary of State and said, "An Ethiopian official, after he had heard the Gospel, said to the evangelist Philip, 'What doth hinder me to be baptized?' I ask, will you also become a Christian?" He answered, "I will." "When will you receive baptism and join the church?" His prompt response was, "Next Sunday." On the following day this fearless man took the chair at the public meeting and stated that he had decided to become a Christian. Even the non-Christians broke into applause when he made this bold statement. On Sunday he was baptized and for some years courageously witnessed as a Christian.

The tide rose still higher in Foochow when I returned in response to a joint invitation from the Governor, the Chamber of Commerce, the Minister of Education, and the Confucian principals of the government colleges. On the night before the meetings were to begin, the interpreter and I went to pray in the quiet cemetery where the missionary martyrs of Foochow lay buried—eleven graves of those who had been torn limb from limb and hacked to pieces by an angry mob less than two decades earlier. Those pioneers who had been counted "foreign devils" had never had the privilege of speaking to an audience of Chinese students, or literati, but I felt that most of the results of our huge meetings were due to the sacrificial lives of those early missionaries and stalwart Chinese Christians.

Sitting on the platform at the first meeting was the aged Archdeacon Wolfe. When he arrived in China fifty-two years before, there were but four Christians in that part of the empire. At the end of our meetings sixteen

hundred students and other young men enrolled themselves as inquirers. What a year of adventure! For five
months, night after night, we faced two thousand, three
thousand, four thousand needy men, and the results were
as tremendous as Brockman had promised.

One of the most significant developments of that year
was a new experiment in organization. With Foochow as
a center we planned a province-wide campaign to carry
the message of Christianity to all parts of the province.
The Confucian Governor and other officials co-operated
with us in assembling the audiences, and we sent out five
teams, each composed of a scientist trained under Robertson and a Christian evangelist. Speaking on science and
religion they addressed tens of thousands throughout this
province of twenty million inhabitants. This nation, that
in the relatively recent Boxer rebellion of 1900 had tried
to wipe out Christianity, had now suddenly become the
greatest field for student evangelism ever known in all
history.

After America was drawn into the First World War,
both the tempo and the mood of China changed. The
Chinese nation was pro-Ally, the Chinese people pro-
American. Thousands of Chinese workingmen went to
Europe to dig trenches. But the peace was disillusioning,
for the Japanese were awarded the former German concessions, including the port of Tsingtao, and various Man-
churian interests. Japan laid her famous Twenty-one
Demands upon China, and the Western powers did not
intercede. During the twenties antiforeign feeling grew;
the Chinese began to know their own strength and to

resent foreign concessions, entanglements, preferments, perfidies—even to resent educational and medical services offered by foreigners.

In 1931 I returned to China again. Mukden was the first of twenty cities that were to participate in an evangelistic campaign. On September 18, the second night of the meetings, the city was seized by the Japanese army. About ten-thirty in the evening an explosion occurred followed by the firing of cannon, machine guns, and rifles throughout the night. In the morning, when we came out of our house, we found that the Japanese had launched a military offensive which, within a few hours, had seized five strategic centers in South Manchuria, although the Japanese had the effrontery to pretend that the Chinese had made the first attack.

All further lectures or meetings were prohibited by the Japanese, and as there was shooting in the streets every night, I proceeded by airplane from Manchuria to Korea and then to Tientsin in China, just as the Council of the League of Nations was about to convene at Geneva. Because I was the only foreigner who had been present at the capture of Mukden free to tell the facts to the world, I sent the following cable on the night of October 12 to Geneva, London, Washington, and Nanking:

I was present at the capture of Mukden. Evidence of many witnesses interviewed at the time and on the spot points to a premeditated, carefully prepared offensive plan of the Japanese army, without the provocation of any Chinese attack, producing bitter resentment when China is already suffering with flood disaster and the world is preoccupied. Japanese troops have not been withdrawn, but all strategic points in South Manchuria are still held by Japanese, and Chinchow also has been bombed.

I testify to evidence of efforts to establish puppet-independence governments in Manchuria under Japanese military control. I have forwarded sworn statements of interviews with Chinese leaders in Mukden who testify to repeated pressure of the Japanese to induce them to head independence governments. Universal indignation in China is taking the form of an economic boycott which the government cannot control. Situation critical, grave developments imminent. All the Orient is looking to the League of Nations and Kellogg Pact signatories for action. Asia believes the League and Pact are on trial as well as Japan and China.

A notable turning toward Soviet Russia as an ally and Communism is developing [italics added], pointing toward the fall of the Nanking Government and widespread Communist anarchy, if the League and Pact fail in this supreme crisis and menace of war.

Mr. Alfred Sze, China's representative at Geneva, read this cable to the Council of the League of Nations.

During my tour of China that year, in a score of cities Communist students were present in almost every meeting. Communism was already rising. In Peiping, one of the first cities visited, some five thousand students a day were in attendance. In the second meeting as I was warning the students against a fatal resort to war with Japan in Manchuria, I referred to Gandhi as one who was winning a great moral and political victory without resort to violence. Instantly, as at an agreed signal, a hundred Communists, hating even the mention of Gandhi, spring up at the back of the hall and began shouting, "Down with this running dog of imperialism," "Down with capitalism," and similar slogans, coupled with obscene epithets.

At once pandemonium broke loose in the hall. The leaders of some two thousand non-Communist students rose and shouted, "Down with the Communists!" and added equally obscene epithets. Communist students poured out the rear of the hall, trying to stampede the meeting, but the rest of the students applauded us, took their seats again, and settled down quietly, and I finished the evening lecture.

That year I also visited the Communist-dominated provinces of South and Central China, including Kiangsi and Hupeh. The rising tide of Communism appalled me. It seemed an alien tide rushing in to inundate the good ancient soil of Chinese democracy, for China at the village level has long been democratic. I did not feel that Communism, Russian variety, could ever lure the Chinese mind, for the Chinese have always credited that government as best which governed least ostentatiously, and Communist government was nothing if not conspicuous, stringent, highhanded. But of course at that time the Chinese had never seen Communist government in action. They merely heard Communist promises and saw the modified Communism which marked a shift in power in certain areas. To them it appeared that the new broom swept clean, as is the way of new brooms, and they expected no better performance than other shifts in power had temporarily effected. China, like most of the rest of the world, was then as much curious as partisan or antagonistic to Communism. There was no long or widespread record to consult. But to a Westerner who knew every section of Asia, as I did, and who knew the vulnerability of students who wished to be free of every form of foreign control, and the resentment of common people newly literate, newly self-conscious, there was definitely menace in the air.

As late as 1935 we conducted a four-month campaign

in China in twenty cities in the twelve crowded provinces which included three-fourths of China's teeming population. By that time new China appeared to be moving at headlong speed. To keep my appointments I made eleven journeys by airplane, most of the planes provided by Generalissimo Chiang Kai-shek, or by the officials or governors of the provinces.

An average of two thousand students a day attended the meetings in these twenty cities. In eight provinces the officials were willing to assemble, usually at the call of the Governor of the province to hear a message on the social and moral evils of the day, including their own graft, which was eating like a cancer into China's national life. Bribery and corruption were rampant, and the widespread use of opium and of the more deadly Japanese drugs was menacing. Sin, personal and social, was an oppressive and deadly fact which could not be escaped.

Having worked out our approach through repeated conferences with missionaries and Chinese leaders we usually spoke the first night on China's sin and desperate need, the second night on God, the third on Christ. These topics were announced as "The Crisis in China," "The Need of China," and "The Hope of China." This series was followed by a decision meeting at which all who had studied in mission colleges or who knew enough of Christianity to make an intelligent decision were permitted to make a final declaration. The new inquirers could then enroll for a six-months study of the New Testament, and Bible classes were organized on the spot with teachers long prepared to lead them.

In the 1935 campaign we came at last to the old city

of Amoy. The chair was taken by the mayor, who on one of my former visits had become an earnest Christian. Another of our workers had come from the very bottom of the social scale. He was a former bandit and opium smoker named Ling-Po who had been changed as if by a moral miracle on a previous occasion. That earlier series of meetings had been held in a large pavilion especially constructed to hold the five thousand students who were admitted by tickets secured only upon written application. This bandit wanted to attend the meetings but, being unable even to sign his name, he could not secure a ticket, nor would he have dared to give his name even if he had been able to write. Accordingly, out of curiosity he cut a hole through the side of the temporary structure so that he could peek through and hear at least fragments of the address.

On the second night he begged a ticket from a student and got inside. He says now that he was convicted of sin as he heard my repeated statement: "The robbers must stop robbing China." We were referring, of course, to the grafting officials, but this bandit applied the message to himself. He knew that he had been robbing China and considered himself even worse than the corrupt officials. At that time he had been an opium smoker and gambler for twenty years and for a decade he had been a leader of some eighty desperadoes. As pirates they boarded the ships in the harbor, as robbers they looted the city, and as bandits they ravaged the countryside. There was a reward of $1,000 for his capture dead or alive.

In the final meeting when we asked how many would turn from their sinful past and enter the new way of life, he rose with the rest, deeply convicted of sin. After being long kept on probation he was finally baptized by the aged Chinese pastor, became a humble evangelist, and for many years raised his own modest support of $10 a month. His first "call" had been to go out as a special worker to reach other bandits, and he won over a hundred and seventy of these gangsters and their neighbors to the Christian life.

Now in this second series of meetings in Amoy he bore witness to Christ in the large public sessions, speaking with tremendous power in meeting after meeting so that the amazed students broke into enthusiastic applause as they saw this moral miracle of a transformed life. It was as real as the transformation of Saul of Tarsus after his enlightenment on the road to Damascus. He offered to give himself up to the authorities and submit not only to prison but to the death sentence for his former crimes. I took the responsibility of asking him not to do so under China's archaic penal system. He finally became the leading evangelist in his province of twenty million people.

During this 1935 campaign in China there was a total attendance of 180,600; 2,476 non-Christians registered their personal decision to enter the Christian life, and 4,144 were enrolled in Bible classes as inquirers to study the New Testament for six months in preparation for making their final decision.

These evangelistic campaigns in China covered just four decades, 1908–1948. So far as I know, never before or since in history have non-Christian students and government officials gathered in such numbers, with thousands on the verge of the great religious decision of their

lives. It looked for a time as if the Christian forces were
going to win the leaders of China and it would become
a Christian nation. Why did we fail in China—or did we
fail? Some of those students and officials who became
Christians or were influenced by Christianity are now
leaders in Formosa. Some are the leaven of the church
in Red China. Some tried to live out their new-found
religion in their daily lives and are dead. Some, let us
admit, were stirred to demand social justice but lacked
the experience to form pressure groups so that, without
sufficient Christian leadership, they fell prey to Communist promises.

Perhaps the most subtle factor working against widespread adoption of Christianity was the fact that Christianity came from the West, as did imperialism; in
repudiating imperialism the emotional thrust also repudiated the religion of the West. Every schoolboy knew it
was the greed of Western imperialism which opened China
by successive opium wars and threatened the partition
of the country among the great powers. For a time forty-
seven of China's chief cities were held in whole or part
by foreign powers. Imperialism brought destruction by
two world wars and opened the way for Japan to invade
China. To the Chinese it seems that today this same imperialism bears the threat of atomic war.

A second factor operating against the widespread
acceptance of Christianity was the refusal of Chiang Kai-
shek, a professed Christian, to make deeply needed reforms. He had the opportunity of establishing the landless
on their beloved soil, but for all practical purposes he
sided with the rich landlords, merchants, generals. Like-

wise he refused to stop the rising tide of graft in which a fantastic inflation was rooted. Perhaps he was unable to do so, for the very men he would have had to offend were politically necessary to him in his wars against Japan and Communism. Wherever the fault lay the fact of governmental disintegration mitigated against the spread of Christianity.

A third factor antagonistic to the spread of Christianity was, of course, the rise of Communism itself. History will have to decide whether the ineptitude of Chiang's armies stemmed from graft and self-aggrandizement within the country or from unwise pressures and vacillating policies among Chiang's foreign allies and advisers. In either case, the Nationalist forces were ineffective. The Communist armies, plus Communist propaganda, promises, and—frankly—performance in behalf of "the people's livelihood," triumphed. And, ostensibly, still triumph.

A final factor operating against widespread acceptance of Christianity was the failure of the church to achieve a disciplined, dedicated leadership among the body of professed followers of Jesus. Perhaps the odds were too great against the infinitesimal Christian minority. And when non-Christians looked to the so-called Christian countries, the United States, Europe, or Latin America, they saw too many characteristics they did not want. Where was any compelling reason for accepting the same way of life?

When I went to the mission field some sixty years ago I believed I carried "good news" for both individuals and nations. At Princeton I had once for all repudiated a message of fear, refusing to believe that all the "heathen" were lost and doomed to eternal punishment by a God of wrath from which Christianity alone could save them. Still, I honestly expected that the whole world would be Christianized, at least nominally, as Europe and America had been. However, when I found Gandhi, a Hindu, to possess a more Christlike character than any national or ecclesiastical leader in the West, I had to ask myself what good baptism or nominal Christianity would do him, either in this world or in the next. Was he not already a son of God, among the "other sheep not of this fold"?

Never in my life have I believed more firmly in missions than I do today. I am glad that Pitkin, Luce, and I made the major choice of our lives and went to Asia—one as a martyr, one as an educator, and one as a lay evangelist. I have seen Christianity make a unique, a priceless contribution to every land in the Orient—and, what is more important, to all the other religions of the world. I believe that the spread of the Gospel of Jesus Christ is necessary for the coming of the Kingdom, or rule of God, whether within history or beyond it. To my last breath I shall make the same fervent appeal for missionaries "in this generation" that I made to the last generation. Missions are as imperative today as they were in the first century or the nineteenth century.

But missions are not enough; the "one sent" represents the body of men who send him, and if the senders are not really dedicated to the Christian way of life, their seeming national hypocrisy will make the Gospel message "sounding brass or clanging cymbals." The world is still dying without the knowledge of the love of God as revealed in Jesus, but it has become crystal clear that the same love which the missionary takes to the uttermost parts of the earth must be the controlling power in the lives of men who profess Christianity at home. Nominal Christianity in America can never supply the need of a world crying for something better than it now knows. God may find a way of answering the need without us, but we can never find a way without him. There is still the missionary imperative for this generation.

Chapter 4

"THE WORLD IN THIS GENERATION"

There have been a few crucial moments that have shaped my whole later life. One was the quiet evening, in 1893, in Union Theological Seminary when I signed the Student Volunteer declaration card. "It is my purpose if God permit to become a foreign missionary." At that moment I *became* a missionary, and urged on by the imperative "in *this* generation" I began to seek a hundred other men to go with me to the foreign field. Not only did this purpose carry me to the mission field but through the years it made me consistently work for volunteers for mission service among the students of the world. At intervals spanning more than six decades I have conducted meetings for the "evangelization of the world" in thirty lands—in every country in Asia that had modern students and in a dozen countries in Europe, as well as in the United States and Canada.

Speaking in foreign countries I had to rely upon interpreters and I soon discovered that there were powerful advantages in this method, because every word came "out of the mouth of two witnesses"—the foreigner whose new message the awakened students were eager to hear and their own trusted leader and patriot who as an interpreter endorsed the message. Obviously, I chose interpreters who were in accord with my message, a very important consideration. By going over the subject in advance, leaving out all the frills, then giving the message in short, staccato sentences, I discovered that an address which would normally take an hour in English could be delivered and interpreted in an hour and ten minutes. I found that in countries like Russia and China audiences could often be held in a solid grip for three successive hours, although given the opportunity to leave at the end of each hour.

In 1911 when the Chinese revolution under Sun Yat-sen temporarily closed the door to the Far East, Baron Nicolai and the Russian student movement invited me to hold meetings in St. Petersburg, Moscow, and Kiev in Czarist Russia. In St. Petersburg the YMCA had erected a building called the *mayak*, or lighthouse, and the Czar was contributing five thousand rubles annually to our work there. However, a YMCA with its social services was one thing and Christian evangelistic services quite another.

In 1912 we began our tour of Russia at Kiev, "the mother of cities" and the ancient center of Russian history. Though we were not able to secure a large theater, night after night some four hundred students crowded into the largest lecture hall available, many of them standing for two hours throughout the lecture. It was a novel experience to conduct meetings with representatives of a hostile government, police, priests, and ecclesiastical authorities of the Orthodox Church present to scrutinize closely every move we made. Although the priests protested against our meetings, the Governor-General protected us and gave us permits. At the close of the Kiev meetings more than sixty students joined Bible classes.

We then went to St. Petersburg, where we had opposition from both the Russian church and state. Baron Nicolai, our interpreter, had to furnish an outline of every lecture, and a police officer in full regimentals sat in a front seat to see that we kept to our outline. No handbills were permitted, and the police struck from the posters any reference to students or to the World Christian Student Movement. In Moscow we were granted no halls, no permits, no printing privilege, and all meetings were forbidden to us by the Czarist officials. Accordingly we had to conduct our meetings in secret. We obtained two large adjacent student rooms and by standing in the doorway between them we could reach two hundred students a night—a hundred crowded together on the floor of each room. After two hours of speaking we would sometimes say: "We must close for tonight, but we will stay for an after-meeting for all who are contemplating suicide." Five or ten students would remain and say quite frankly they found life impossible in Czarist Russia and were being driven to the extremity of taking their own lives. One Jewish student wrote me: "I have not met among our young people a single thoughtful man who has not at one time or another contemplated suicide."

At our meetings in Moscow there was a girl, a medical student, who saw the announcement of our lecture on "The Meaning of Life." As she stood sneering before this poster she wondered what the foreign speaker could possibly have to say upon this subject; she then decided to postpone the hour of her death at least until the con-

clusion of that lecture. While still in Russia I received this
letter from her:

> I am a medical student troubled by doubts and passions. I had
> lost all faith and saw no meaning in life. I decided to put an end to
> my days by suicide, and day and night I thought of committing it.
> On the 25th of January I left my friend for the last time, saying,
> "Good-bye; tomorrow I will cease to exist." A life without meaning,
> without aim, without eternity, with nothing but human pleasures,
> was disgusting to me. It was then that I saw the notice of your
> lectures on "The Meaning of Life" and "A Rational Basis for
> Religion." I went, and on returning, I went to sleep for the first
> time in two months without thought of suicide. After that night I
> attended all your lectures. I now read the Bible daily and am again
> able to pray. I do not know what the future will be, but now I desire
> again to live. In any case, I shall prolong my life for the next three
> months to make the test of Jesus Christ by reading the Gospels once
> more and making the experiment which you suggested. Pray for me.

I knew that there were skeptics, atheists, and students
contemplating suicide in every meeting. I therefore made
them this challenge: "I do not ask for blind credulity,
nor that you try to swallow all that I have said. I only ask
you to make an experiment which is as reasonable and
scientific as any in the chemical laboratory: 'If any one
will *do*, he shall *know*' (John 7:17). If you will read
through any one of the four Gospels, studying a small
portion each day for three months with open mind, and
will honestly try to put into practice what you do believe,
whatever appeals to your own reason and conscience as
true, I challenge you and claim that you will find God a
growing spiritual reality in your life before you have completed that experiment."

With many others, this medical student believed that

this was a fair test. She walked miles through the snow to a Bible class taught by our second interpreter, Madame Poika. This able woman, a friend of many of the nobility, had herself found Christ as a mighty spiritual reality when, as a thoughtless young society girl, she had attended Moody's evangelistic meetings in London. I learned later in a letter from Baron Nicolai that the medical student finally found God for herself and was on her way to relieve the famine sufferers of Russia.

In countless instances we saw God at work among the despairing students and among the young revolutionary students, in spite of the almost insurmountable handicaps of a discredited church and a tyrannical state, which many students considered to be the worst enemies of the people. This was the Czarist "Holy Russia" we knew in 1912.

In 1921 I had the thrilling adventure of facing large audiences of awakened students in Egypt and Turkey. Those were amazing meetings in Egypt, where I worked in co-operation with Samuel Zwemer and William Gairdner of Oxford, with Sheik Mitri as the marvelous interpreter. We had huge gatherings in four centers from Upper Egypt to the delta. In Cairo the newly awakened youth, both Moslems and Copts, filled three meetings in succession each night, as the students often did in China and Russia. Each evening I spoke first in a theater filled with hundreds of Egyptian women; then in another larger theater, the Kursaal, filled with two thousand men, and then in the American Mission Church to students who had come from the two earlier meetings for rapid-fire questions on the particular phase of Christianity on which

I had been speaking. Our wonderful interpreter, Sheik
Mitri, gave the message with speed and fire in perfect
Arabic. Time and again on some moral issue the audience
would break into a storm of applause. On the closing night
hundreds of men signed cards; during the week over a
thousand signed as inquirers.

From Cairo we went to Tanta, Assiut, and Luxor. At
Assiut, in Upper Egypt, we held from three to seven meetings a day for five days. We met in a great tent and by
means of a sounding board everyone could hear perfectly.
Every morning an average of three thousand attended a
Bible class, and on the last morning six thousand Christians gathered. The evening meetings were evangelistic,
for Moslems, Copts, and nominal Christians, and the audience averaged six or seven thousand a night. Many hundreds of them signed cards promising daily to read the
Scriptures, daily to pray, especially for Moslems, and to
seek to win them to Christ.

In 1929, eight years after my first visit to Turkey, I
went back again and found a new republic in the place
of the corrupt and tottering Ottoman Empire. Formerly I
had seen the last of the Sultans review his troops in Con-
stantinople and had met the Sheik ul Islam and the proud
heads of the old bigoted religious hierarchy. But the first
few months after the First World War witnessed the
brilliant rise of Mustafa Kemal, who drove five foreign
armies from his soil and at Lausanne wrested a diplomatic
victory from the proud Lord Curzon and the diplomats
of Europe. Through flaming Turkish nationalism Kemal
Pasha made a score of revolutionary changes: on a single
day the new Roman alphabet replaced the old classic

Arabic which had bound Turkey to Asia and to the past;
a new educational system was introduced, and women
were liberated from their seclusion, including their veils.
I watched the beginnings of a new agriculture, industry,
and trade for the once indolent and impractical Turks.
I saw the fearless Kemal Pasha abolish at one stroke the
sultanate and the caliphate, under which the Turks had
long led the forces of Islam to war. Thereafter mosques
became schools between prayer periods.

After thirty centuries of warfare about her straits, and
thirteen centuries of strife between Moslems and Christians, I saw at last the rebirth of Turkey. I was able to
address not only the students of the Imperial Ottoman
University but theaters filled with Turkish Moslem students. What most impressed me was to be asked to speak
in a theater to Turkish women students, all unveiled and
many of them having been released from former Moslem
harems. They were studying to prepare for teaching and
other professions newly opened to them, or to become
homemakers under new laws which for the first time
gave women civil, political, and economic rights.

In no country in Europe was God more evidently at
work transforming lives individually and socially than in
Czechoslovakia. In a strange way I was thrown with the
students and leaders of this land in two of the great crises
of its history.

In 1920 the Czechs had their first student conference,
after three centuries of Hapsburg tyranny under which no
student meetings of any kind on religious, political, or
social questions had been permitted. They invited me to
come as the foreign guest speaker. I knew enough of their

history to realize that I would be facing many ardent young atheists and rationalists, whose only acquaintance with religion was what they had seen of it under the oppression of the church and state of their conquerors. In the museum in Prague I saw the instruments of torture that had been used in the Inquisition in the effort to stamp out Protestantism. It was no wonder that many of them had rejected the only kind of religion, or pseudo religion, they had ever known.

Soon after World War I Huntley Dupre, an American student secretary of the YMCA, had erected as a community center a large building filled daily with four thousand needy students. After months of prayer and planning he had arranged for this first student conference, hoping that there might be founded, in this once Protestant land of John Huss and the early Reformation, a real Christian Student Movement related to churches which were once more free.

Our conference was held in an old feudal castle at Prerov in Bohemia. In a daily Bible class we began the study of the Sermon on the Mount. Some of the Czechs had never read or even seen a Bible. Here were atheists, agnostics, nominal Catholics, Protestants, and many who were indifferent or violently antireligious. Almost from the beginning we could see God at work. The Bible came to these young people as a new book, a challenging moral discovery. It was literally like dynamite. We were soon witnessing moral miracles, as students were finding God for the first time in their lives. Nor was their concept of religion a selfish, personal, possessive salvation merely for their own souls in some future life. They had a country to save, a new nation to build, a people to Christianize again and to vitalize in all the relationships of life, religious, social, and political. Many of them began to seek first the Kingdom of God and to enter in at the straight gate and narrow way as they studied for the first time this marvelous Sermon on the Mount. I have never been a literalist and I have often observed that "the letter killeth" whether among Pharisees or Christians, but in that conference through a fresh study of the New Testament I saw, as I have often done among inquirers from the non-Christian religions, that the flaming Word of God, as Karl Barth would say, was "living and active and sharper than a two-edged sword."

Then something happened that staggered us as Christians and tested our faith. The students called upon the popular Minister of Education to address the group, and he made in his address a scathing attack upon all religion as reactionary, superstitious, and unscientific. The atheists rallied and claimed a victory. They demanded a debate between this cabinet member, as a rationalistic atheist, and myself as a believer. As we left the hall I remember turning to my friend, Huntley Dupre, and saying: "Huntley, let us not be afraid; God is not dead; we are not beaten."

The next day most of the students went out as usual for the afternoon sports and games and then went down to take their plunge in the Elbe River at the end of the day. Suddenly an alarm was sounded—one of them had been drowned and could not be revived. Those students, many of them atheists, brought up that dead body, and here was a problem on their hands. They had to have some kind of funeral service for decency's sake. Otherwise, the already indignant peasants in the neighborhood would have accused them of godlessness. But because of their prejudice the students would call no minister, or priest, or rabbi to conduct a religious service. So they asked me as a layman and engineer to conduct some kind of service. Out there in the dust of the road we stood about the coffin before the body was sent away to Moravia to the boy's sorrowing parents, who were poor peasants.

Facing that student conference over the coffin I said: "Fellow students, what have we here in this coffin—only a hundred and fifty pounds or more of flesh? Is there no soul, no God, no life beyond, no hope for this poor boy or his sorrowing parents? Has he died like a dog, 'without hope and without God'? Must we send home with this dead body the death of all their hopes to his poor father and mother, who have sacrificed for a lifetime to give their boy an education in the university?

"Or, if there is a God, a soul, a life beyond, a larger, expanding, glorious life into which this boy has already entered, then all things are possible for this boy and for every one of us." Then to their amazement I opened an unfinished letter found in the pocket of his coat left on the shore. Unknown to us, he was one of the daily growing group that had already found God and had entered into life. He had begun writing to a friend: "Dear ———, I have found a new experience, a new life. I see no hope for the world but the love of Christ. A great task awaits the students of our land. I for one must be a better man. It is possible . . ."

At that point in the letter had come the call: "All out

for the games, fellows, come on." He had hastily folded the unfinished letter, thrust it in his pocket, rushed out to the games and then to swim. I cannot describe the impression of that letter upon the students. It was like an electric shock. They felt somehow that this boy was alive and speaking to them, not from that closed coffin but, as it were, from an open heaven. I took as my text for that funeral sermon the closing words of his unfinished sentence, "It is possible." I said:

Fellow students, when I came to this conference, the first that you have ever held in this new republic, I came here in the faith held by John Huss. For three centuries you have been able to hold no such meetings as these, but now you are again free and able to build your new republic. When I put that New Testament into your hands on the first day, because of your prejudice I called it the book of John Huss. I believed that the spirit of your great Bohemian martyr would influence this conference, and that Jesus Christ, once crucified, but now risen and alive forever more, would speak here and raise men who were spiritually dead. I think he has been doing it. I believed that this Bible, forbidden by the church for a hundred and fifty years, would speak again as a living Word.

I came to this conference in the faith that not less than twelve of you, like apostles, would step out to rekindle the fires of freedom and of faith in this country of John Huss, in ancient Bohemia and Moravia, the lands of the Christian martyrs. Now I want to ask every student here one question. I do not ask if you are a Catholic or Protestant, a churchman or non-churchman, an atheist or believer. Whatever your allegiance, *it is possible* for every one of you to find God. *It is possible* to build a new Republic of Czechoslovakia that may some day carry out all the dreams of John Huss which were frustrated or postponed when he was burned at the stake. It is possible to found a Christian Student Movement, to enter into fellowship with the World's Student Christian Federation where ancient Bohemia may again take her honored place in the religious

world. *It is possible* that you too may have a part in the building of
a new world that shall hold as its ideal the Kingdom of God on
earth. My one question is: "Are you going to be one of the twelve?"
It is possible for *you.*

As the boy's body was carried away that evening in the
little YMCA Ford truck, those students who as yet knew
no religious hymn sang their Czech folk song: "Good
Night, Sleep Well." On the last day at the closing meeting the daughter of the cabinet member who had cut their
faith from under the feet of some of them took the chair.
Every student in turn rose to speak of his experience at
the conference. Not twelve but more than twice twelve
took their stand for God and Christ. Three atheists became honest inquirers. After that meeting the leaders
founded a Christian Student Movement for Czechoslovakia, and they entered the membership of the World's
Student Christian Federation as "The Czechoslovak Student Renaissance Movement."

Every meeting in a foreign country whether in Asia or
Europe was an adventure, but so were meetings in the
colleges of the United States and Canada. During the
years I was asked to take "religious emphasis weeks" or
evangelistic campaigns in several hundred colleges. An
account of one of these early campaigns in the University
of California lies before me in a letter written in March,
1914. Such a campaign was a new thing on the hard-
boiled "gold coast" of California, but the students wanted
one and had asked me to come and conduct it. The student committee responsible for the meetings was thoroughly representative of the California spirit of the time,
including agnostics, Protestants, and Catholics. The stu-

dent responsible for the publicity was an agnostic but with great efficiency he reached the whole campus through the college daily. The redheaded university cheerleader got behind the movement and announced to his fraternity brothers, "Fellows, this bird sure has a wicked line of chatter; you simply must come out and hear him." They came. Some sixteen hundred men turned out each night, with growing interest right to the end of the meetings.

The Christian chairman of the campaign committee had just been released from jail for forging a check while drunk the previous week. He was the most earnest man on the campus and stood by me through thick and thin. He said that he knew "damned well" that *he* needed genuine conversion and he thought the whole university probably did.

The day before starting for California I had received a letter from the student committee which placed me in a straitjacket. It set forth the conditions imposed by the timid president of the university, who was mortally afraid of offending either Jews or Gentiles, Catholics or Protestants, religionists or anti-religionists on the campus. The students informed me that the president had finally consented to allow us to use the university gymnasium, but there must be no prayers, no singing of hymns, no worship; there must be no discussion of controversial subjects, and no decisions or commitments. Furthermore, we could not leave the campus to go to any neighboring church or other building to do any of these things. The meetings had already been announced and it was too late to cancel the engagement, so we had to begin under these conditions.

One night after one of the meetings a student came up

and asked, "Where could I buy those four books you advised us to read?" I replied that, although I frequently recommended books, I had not done so that night. When he continued to insist that I had, I said: "You surely don't mean my allusion to the four Gospels, Matthew, Mark, Luke and John?" "Yes," he said, brightening, "where could I buy those books?" I turned him over to the fine Catholic priest who was in the campaign with us up to the hilt, and he enrolled the student in his Bible class.

As we approached the end of the meetings, I said to the committee: "There has evidently been a new and unprecedented interest on the campus in the whole subject of religion and in clean living. Many have decided to eliminate certain habits and to lead new lives. If you do not know who these men are, you will be unable to help them; in a week or two most of them will be back in the old habits and relationships, and the meetings will have been useless so far as they are concerned."

The committee decided unanimously that we should give the men a chance to come to a decision or to express their new purpose so that we could unite them and help them, and at the request of the student committee the university president reluctantly consented to the plan. Though there was no emotionalism and no putting men in a corner under pressure, of some sixteen hundred in attendance on the last night, twelve hundred remained for a second meeting. About four hundred of these signified their interest by signing cards, either as inquirers or as promising to study the four Gospels. Over a hundred men made the decision to become Christians, including the agnostic who had been responsible for the publicity.

This student gathering was typical of others held at the time at Leland Stanford, the University of Chicago, Yale, Princeton, and other colleges and universities. The campus response to religion varies with student generations. Today college students are not as responsive as they were in the period when our meetings were part of the great student movement that included practically all parts of the world. There is a different religious atmosphere now. Perhaps not a less acute concern with spiritual growth, and perhaps an even greater social sensitivity, but the mood is very different from that of the years before America entered the First World War.

As I look back over the decades I can now clearly see something which we only sensed at the time—the profound spiritual power generated by the conventions of the Student Volunteer Movement held every four years. The Protestant Church has no spiritual orders calling for vows of poverty, chastity, and obedience such as the Catholic Church has had through the centuries. But Protestant young people have always had the same eagerness to dedicate their lives to a cause that calls for supreme sacrifice. The missionary movement became that cause. When some five thousand of the best-endowed young people of American colleges were gathered in a Student Volunteer convention under the spiritual leadership of that day there was created a unique spiritual power that those who attended could never forget. Lives were changed for all time and history was made for distant lands.

Two men towered over those gatherings. The first was the chairman, John R. Mott, the great Christian organizer and statesman of the nineteenth century. Mott was called in his day the "master of assemblies." The other man was

Robert E. Speer, an early secretary of the Student Volunteer Movement and later secretary of the Presbyterian Board of Foreign Missions. His was the prophetic voice, speaking with searching power to the Student Volunteers of America and on his periodic world tours to all Protestant missionaries and Christians. Both of these men knew the world they lived in; they traveled constantly; Europe and Asia were their neighborhoods and they knew their neighbors, the great and illustrious, but also the poor, the inarticulate, the harassed. Night after night they could speak to the same audience or to widely varied audiences and never repeat a single incident or illustration. One factor which gave their addresses dimension was their wealth of unused material; their experience far outran their best presentation so that everything they said had validity, expanse, drive. But greater than their knowledge of events and movements was their insight born of the experience of God. They had tried him and knew his power and they poured out that power with authority. It swept through an audience, awakening and regraining personality so that men and women could stand up and pledge themselves to the future with conviction and strength. From these Student Volunteer conventions, as from the day of Pentecost, came the missionaries of the student generation of the nineteenth century—the great missionary century of all time.[1]

[1] The editor feels that a footnote is here imperative. Sherwood Eddy was the third member of this great "triumvirate." His was a prophetic voice both in America and in Asia; he was among the first advocates of the social gospel in its entirety, an emphasis which supplemented the individual personal message of the earlier years under Moody. Students responded wholeheartedly and in large numbers to his conviction that only in this complete application could Christianity effectively challenge the modern world.

Chapter 5

❦

THE PROBLEM OF WAR

When World War I broke out, the Allies were as unprepared to deal with soldier morale and morals as they were to meet the enemy on the battlefield. I was then forty-seven years old, overage so far as the military draft was concerned, and I felt that I could render my largest service as a noncombatant. I felt that my years of experience with large meetings might be turned to good account in work with the men in the fighting forces. So I went to Europe at the invitation of the British YMCA on behalf of the British army and began work with a series of nightly meetings in some sixty YMCA huts on Salisbury Plain. After a hard day of drilling and marching, men would saunter in, Captain "Peg" would start some singing, and in a few minutes tired faces would relax. Then I would talk to the crowd. I shared all that I had with these men, night after night, in camps all over England, Wales, and Scotland.

In 1917, a month after America's entrance into the war, I returned to the States but soon sailed again for the war zone. This time I took a party of ten evangelists to speak to the soldiers in the British army and sixty students from Northwestern and Princeton universities for

work in the British Y huts. The group of speakers included
Merton Rice, Burris Jenkins, Henry Crane, and Walter
Sherman.

At that time there was friction and misunderstanding
between the veteran Allied troops and our newly arrived,
boasting American soldiers. To help ease the tension I was
sent with a deputation of four Americans to accompany a
British staff officer along the whole Allied front in Belgium and France from Ypres to Verdun. Lloyd George,
as Prime Minister of Britain, had arranged this expedition
so that we might tell American divisions of the spirit, the
traditions, and the magnitude of the effort of the war-
weary Allied armies, hoping that a greater measure of
appreciation among the American troops would result
from this awareness. Like a trip through Dante's *Inferno*
we went down the long line from the trenches in Belgium
to the Somme, then to Rheims, which we watched under
fire, and finally to the great fortress at Verdun where we
dined in the rock underground with the French command
in front of the proud motto, "They shall not pass."

The scenes along the battle front were terrible. At one
time I wrote:

The ground has been fought over inch by inch and foot by foot.
It is blasted and blackened; lifeless trees stand on the bare ridge,
stiff and stark. Small villages are left without one stone or brick upon
another, mere formless heaps of dust and debris. Here the battle has
raged on three levels, in the air, on the land and in the mines in the
bowels of the earth, with all the forces of the cyclone and earthquake
harnessed for destruction. I thrilled at the sound of the mighty and
unearthly forces loosed, until suddenly I realized that all about me
men were dying. Between us and the enemy was just one deep
trench and a thin red line of flesh and blood as a human rampart.

Among the fighting men whom I met in France was Sapper Wright of western Canada, who had just been through the underground battle for the capture of Messines ridge. In graphic description he said:

Well, sir, we were digging under Hill 60. A shell exploded and buried us all; three of us were killed and two were still alive, buried there for seven hours till they finally dug us out, unconscious. Then we started another sap [trench] to lay a mine. I was listening to the approach of the enemy's sappers when suddenly they were on us! We killed seven and took the rest of the twenty Germans prisoners and then crawled through and blew up their sap.

You say, was I a Christian, or did religion mean anything to me in this hell? Not me! I was wild and going to the devil. Then one night I was wounded and lay in a deserted shell hole, shot through the thigh and unable to move for fifteen hours, thinking my end had come. I was feeling for a cigarette in my pocket to ease the pain a bit, but no luck. All I could find was a little pocket Testament given me in the Y hut, but which I'd never read. I managed to wrench it out, and thinking that I might never be found and that this was probably my last hour, I started to read it to try to forget my wound. By accident the book fell open at the twenty-seventh chapter of Matthew, about Christ dying on the cross and Pilate's question, "What then shall I do with Jesus who is called Christ?"

Well, sir, that changed my life and I have read a chapter of that Book every day since then. I was finally picked up by the infantry and carried to the hospital. I'm a different man now. I'm off to the front tomorrow to take my turn again, but I'm no longer alone nor afraid up there in the trenches.

One night I was with a group of tommies belonging to the Black Watch when the question was asked as to the bravest act they had seen during the entire war. One man replied:

There were about twenty of us in the trench when the Germans threw in a bomb. In a second or two some of us would be blown to pieces. Then like a flash, for there was no time to think, the best man among us threw himself on the bomb as if it had been a football, to take the death and break the force of the explosion for the rest of us. There was a roar and then silence. We went to pick him up and he was still breathing. Later they dug countless fragments of that bomb out of his two legs but he was still living. A score of us walked out of that trench that night unharmed because of this man.

I also held meetings in all the larger venereal hospitals. At one of these base hospitals the commanding officer told me that in this hospital alone over eighty thousand men incapacitated by venereal disease had been treated. I saw the significance of venereal disease both from a moral and from a military point of view. When General Pershing arrived in France with the first divisions from America I laid before him my plan for meeting the problem. However, he was interested only in physical, not moral, prophylaxis and did not welcome the plan. Like Lord Kitchener he belonged to the hard-boiled old school that wanted an efficient fighting force and nothing more, and that is what we got.

My job during the war was to offer religion—a hope, an anchorage, a moral dynamic—to fighting men, living and dying. I spoke to audiences of three hundred to a thousand men every night and, after I joined the newly arrived American forces in France, sometimes to many hundreds during the day in meetings out in the fields between their periods of drill. Dwight L. Moody once said that the Civil War was his university. The First World War was that for some of us.

The greatest man in YMCA work in France was Joey Callan, who conducted work in thirty huge war huts filled each night with sixty thousand British soldiers in the great

base camp in Rouen. I was among the staff of workers
and lecturers who periodically visited this and other British base camps in France. Our team of speakers included
men of varied professional interests: Professor Bateson,
the great biologist of Cambridge; Professor Burkett, New
Testament scholar; Professor Oman, E. A. Burroughs of
Oxford, Dr. Cairns of Aberdeen, Lord William Gascoyne
Cecil; entertainers like Harry Lauder; and evangelists
like John McNeill and Gypsy Smith. A score of us workers
lived together, worked in the huts by day and spoke to
the men at night. The British High Command believed
in reaching the whole man and wanted us frankly to discuss postwar problems—such as economic justice, racial
brotherhood, and lasting peace—but I found no such
attitude in America in either World War I or World
War II.

I was so moved by the tragedy of the war that I wrote
in Britain a little book, *Suffering and the War*, which was
also printed in paper covers for widespread circulation
among the soldiers. In 1917 I wrote *With Our Soldiers
in France*, interpreting my experiences at the front, endeavoring to enlist support for the war work of the YMCA,
and trying to strengthen public morale.

Periodically during World War I, I returned to the
United States with the story of the sacrifices of the fighting
men, in order to help raise funds for the war welfare work
of the various agencies ministering to the troops, including
the YMCA, the Knights of Columbus, the Salvation Army,
et cetera. On the last drive $200,000,000 was the enor-
mous goal set and reached. With others I spoke in the

Metropolitan Opera House of New York, in theaters between acts, and to mass meetings all over America. We secured some fairly large gifts. When Mott and I had lunch with the railway magnate, Arthur Curtis James, we asked him for a sizable contribution to this fund. After the most abject apologies he said that he was sorry but that at the moment he could give us only half a million! This generous giving was characteristic of many Americans at that time.

The war brought me face to face with one of the supreme moral problems of my life and of my generation. What was I to do about war in the future? I can remember pacing up and down the sands of the seashore in the great base camps of France within sound of the guns, deeply troubled in conscience and wrestling with the most difficult moral problem of my life up to that time. At the end of the war I estimated that it had resulted in the direct and indirect loss of some 30,000,000 lives. We had burned up in ammunition and other costs approximately 337 billions of dollars. The war had often destroyed moral standards and had employed propaganda, true and false, reprisals and counterreprisals, atrocities and counter-atrocities. After long thought I felt driven to take the position of absolute pacifism. While holding this view I wrote *The Abolition of War* and my *Pilgrimage of Ideas,* both long out of print. I spoke on the subject widely and made many converts to the pacifist position, in which I then firmly believed.

Throughout my life I have tried to be honest with ideas. Whatever I believed at any one time I believed firmly;

when experience and my best thinking brought me to a different position I tried to face the necessity of taking a different stand. As a reaction to the monstrous evils of World War I, I accepted the ideal of peace and became for a time an absolute idealist and pacifist in the light of what I then understood to be Jesus' way of life. I believed then with Einstein that if only 2 per cent of us—enough to fill all our prisons and jails—would go on strike against war, refusing to fight under any circumstances, it would mean the abolition of war. In desperation the makers of national policies would have to find some other method of settling disputes.

But when Mussolini seized Abyssinia, when Hitler invaded the Rhineland and a dozen countries thereafter in an attempt to conquer the world, when Japan seized Manchuria and invaded China and southeastern Asia, we found nothing that could stop them except the use of force. We had to work on the given instant with society as it was. To be sure, Gandhi used successfully a different weapon—love, expressed in non-violent resistance—and set India free. But one reason he could succeed was that his enemy, Britain, had a conscience; the British might imprison him for years but could not bring themselves to put him to death. In Russia, however, I saw Tolstoyan non-resisters and in Germany complete pacifists who used the same weapon that Gandhi employed, yet they were completely ineffectual against Stalin and Hitler, who promptly put them to death. I believe that Gandhi would never have been heard from in Russia or Germany.

I now believe that the absolute ethic of Jesus must be maintained as a frame of reference by which every individual and every society must be judged; but I consider an absolute ethic an "impossible possibility" and a false perfectionism when set up as a rigid law—such as absolute pacifism—or when taken as a literal guide to action for all men at all times in all circumstances. Possessing no infallible or specific guide or code of morals that can be clearly applied to all, many of us must take a pragmatic position seeking to establish a tolerable justice and peace under conditions of man's sinfulness. All men are sinful; none is perfect. All human selfishness, of pacifists and nonpacifists alike, is contrary to God's will. Most men have a sound human instinct that refuses to abide by an absolute of nonresistant personal perfectionism, which seems to them absurd. They have a conviction that love requires them to protect the weak against the strong and against any totalitarian aggressor. I have come to feel that for the majority absolute pacifism is a moralistic corruption of the Christian gospel.

I do not expect that World War III or any other war will ever solve our problems. We face a real menace in a desperately real world, where war must be God's patient problem—and ours.[1] How will God solve the problem? Perhaps just as he worked with us to solve the issue of slavery. All through history there are two types of minds: absolute idealists and pragmatists, relativists, realists. These two groups constitute a minority and a majority.

[1] Professor Quincy Wright, in *A Study of War*, shows that in the last 461 years from 1480 to 1941 the various nations took part in wars as follows: Great Britain 78 wars, France 71, Spain 64, Russia 61, Austria 52, Germany 23, China 11, Japan 9; the United States fought 13 wars in 150 years and, in addition, 110 wars were fought, often ruthlessly, against the Indians within the United States. If these are "the peace-loving peoples," who are warmongers?

Slavery was first challenged in England and America by the minority of absolute idealists, such abolitionists as Wilberforce and the harsh, war-provoking extremist William Lloyd Garrison. But slavery was never abolished until such realists and practical men as William Pitt and Abraham Lincoln entered the fray.

The procedure may be the same with war and with every other major moral problem or reform. A few idealists, absolute pacifists and conscientious objectors, who hear the commands—imperative to them—"Thou shalt not kill" and "Ye therefore shall be perfect," will take an absolutist position, disturb men's consciences, and challenge the whole war system. I believe, however, that never until the pragmatists, relativists, and realists act effectively will wars be abolished. I now feel, with Reinhold Niebuhr, Einstein, and more than five thousand other former pacifists in America and Britain, that at the last extremity we are faced by a choice between two gigantic evils, neither of which permits us personal perfection. If another war comes, we must either accept and enter a total, devastating war against the forces of another Hitler or Stalin, or we must accept total slavery, and I could fight with a clear conscience if dragged into such a conflict.

If we are to save our world from atomic destruction we must do away with war. We must build up both world community and world organization, however long the task may take. Working through the United Nations, not impatiently by-passing it or trying as egotistic isolationists to "go it alone," we must achieve a world federally organized for peace. The atomic bomb, however, makes the challenge of the war issue immediate and imperative. To accomplish the goal of world peace I believe that on one hand we need at least a few pacifists as absolute idealists, and on the other hand many realists and relativists. The two forces working in dialectic tension—by the resolution of opposites—will finally do away with the war system. Just as in the early days of our national life Jefferson and Hamilton working in dialectic tension built our economy both in agriculture and in industry, so I believe that idealists and realists, pacifists and nonpacifists must build a world of peace.

I almost envy many absolutists the seeming simplicity of the issue they face, somewhat as follows: God has finally revealed himself in Jesus and his way of life; the social action most contrary to this way of life is war, "the world's chief collective sin"; therefore war is wrong—*all* war always was wrong. All slavery is contrary to Jesus' way of life; therefore all slavery is and always was wrong. If I am an absolutist my duty is plain. I must follow Jesus' way of peace and freedom for myself at all costs, and God, not I, is responsible for the results.

The pragmatist—everywhere under the limitations of historical relativism—may well envy this oversimplification. He finds no verbal infallibility in the Bible. Save a few quotations made by "Matthew" from the original Gospel of Mark, one finds no saying of Jesus recorded in the same words in any two Gospels. Jesus' way of life was unmistakably the way of love, but how was love to be applied in action? Did Jesus apply it, for instance, to the system of slavery? Did he ever try to free the slaves or condemn slavery? Or did Paul regulate the system for masters

and slaves for nineteen centuries to come? After nineteen
long centuries, under the principle of gradual revelation
and growing human understanding, the world's conscience was at last awakened on the subject of slavery. Men
finally saw that Jesus' whole way of life revealed the principles of brotherhood under which slaves should be freed,
educated, and given their full rights as equal brothers.
However, it took many, many centuries to end slavery and
in our segregated society we are still far from realizing the
principles of Jesus in racial brotherhood.

Similarly, did Jesus ever make a clear pronouncement
upon the war system? Did he tell the Roman centurion to
abandon the army? Why was Peter, his chief follower,
carrying a sword on the last night if Jesus had ever condemned the use of force? And what did Jesus mean by
telling his followers each to sell his cloak and buy a sword?
Though it may have been for self-defense, certainly it was
not for his defense. *There is no single clear solution in the
New Testament on which all can agree concerning the use
of force, self-defense, and war.* The possible solutions have
divided Christians for nineteen centuries and will probably divide them for centuries to come. In the last war, in
Great Britain roughly one in 300 registered as a conscientious objector, while 299 of every 300 were conscientious defenders of their country and their threatened way of
life in the free world. The proportion of conscientious objectors was even smaller in America and in other countries.
Of course, truth can never be determined by a majority
vote. When truth was incarnate in its most perfect form it
stood in a minority of one against the world. Unfortunately, the absolutist, the fundamentalist, or the fanatic

always feels that he is right and the rest of the world is wrong. Most of us, however, cannot regard lightly the sound instinct of the majority.

If my conduct is to be regulated by either custom, authority, instinct, reason, or experience, for myself I must select human experience both individual and social, as interpreted by reason. At the summit of human experience I must examine the message of the prophets as consummated in Jesus: "Jesus came into Galilee, preaching the gospel (good news) of God, saying the kingdom of God is at hand, repent and believe in the good news." The good news is ultimately about God; it is that God is love. My joy is to walk in the light of God's love, to love God with my whole heart, and my neighbor—including my enemy—as myself. My joy is to seek the Kingdom, or rule of God, in justice, in equal opportunity for all and in the equal brotherhood of all. This search must eventuate for me in the beatitude of peace, a peace based on a world learning to live, and let live, co-operatively. Achieving such peace may take as long as abolishing slavery took, and will surely take as much time as is required to realize brotherhood.

Because I have come finally to the conclusion that my one duty is to love God, my neighbor, and my enemies, and to do the will of God as I see it in the light that I have, I would join the armed forces in the event of another world war. If I were young enough, I would volunteer for the air force, not because I hate but because I love. If my bombs fell either on the enemy or on innocent civilians, they would only hasten my victims through the portal miscalled death into a better environment, into the presence of the God of all grace. As I see it now, I could have stood beside

Leonidas and his three hundred Spartans at Thermopylae for the defense of all future freedom for Greece and the world. I could have followed Charles Martel in turning back the Moslem hordes from the conquest of Europe. I could have joined Garibaldi and his brave thousand against the tyranny of the old order, and I could have marched with Washington at Valley Forge.

My dear friend, Kirby Page, as an absolute pacifist, believes that he is right and I am wrong in the matter of war, while I, now a pragmatist, relativist and realist, believe that *both positions are right and both are necessary.* I believe that as between the two the absolute pacifist is doing the greater good. It would, however, be a moral wrong for me to become an absolute pacifist today, as it would have been for Abraham Lincoln to become an abolitionist follower of Garrison. Lincoln's call was to save the Union and to stop slavery when he could. All had not the same duty. I hope I can have understanding of my absolutist brother who differs from me as to the means to be used to achieve peace. None of us must ask, "Lord, what shall this other man do?" Each must obey the command, "Follow thou me."

I believe that God who is love is patiently working out through us his long-range problems that stretch over the centuries—war and slavery, justice and brotherhood. I believe that God was working in both Plato and Aristotle, though neither had the whole truth; in both Amos and Hosea, in Paul and Peter, whatever their quarrels; in the historic Synoptics and the later contradictory Fourth Gospel; through the Catholic Augustine and the Protestant Luther. I believe that he is working today in both the conservative and the liberal, the absolutist and the relativist, the fundamentalist and the modernist, the pacifist and the nonpacifist. Each must stand humbly before his own Lord, believing that the only way for him is the way of love as he sees it.

This is my present attitude toward war.

Chapter 6

❦

SEEING LIFE WHOLE

At the World Missionary Conference at Edinburgh in 1910 John R. Mott was called to lead the world missionary movement. Since he was already doing the work of three men, it was necessary for him to unload some of his other duties in order to accept this new responsibility. One of his duties fell to me and resulted in the arrangement that I would act in the capacity of YMCA secretary for Asia but would also spend part of each year in the United States seeking the men and the support needed to carry on the Association work in the Orient. Because of this appointment we returned to America to make our home here.

During these years of solicitation I met men with large hearts and great capacity for giving; I also met men whose generous giving had been crushed by the load of their wealth. Dealing constantly with both sorts, I was led to a serious reappraisal of my own attitude toward the use of money. Upon the death of my father in 1894 the greater part of his estate had been left to my mother, but I had received a small inheritance from it. I now proposed to my mother that she and her three sons agree, literally, never to lay up for themselves another dollar of "treasure on earth." We all gave common consent not to increase our

capital and to give all of our surplus each year to the work
for which we were also giving our lives. Beginning with my
appointment to India in 1896 I have followed the practice
of taking no salary for my work.[1]

This new work of raising money I found to be difficult
and challenging—indeed, as exciting as big-game shooting.
Before some men of wealth I presented a plan similar to
the one I was following and watched their reactions. As I
studied these men—and the society which produced both
the men and the wealth—I began to raise questions about
the existing social order. My experience in the First World
War had increased my awareness of the incompleteness
and inadequacy of the message I was proclaiming. The
conviction formed in my mind that the Christian gospel is
more than good news for individuals in their personal relations; it is also a message about the Kingdom of God and
the way of life for men in their group and corporate
affairs—in economics, politics, international relations, and
all other interrelationships.

As I look back upon my life I can see that this position
was reached by successive steps through which God became real to me in actual experience. The first step was an
individual and personal experience of God, yet it was
solitary. I can remember no sudden experience of conversion in my healthy and happy rearing. In my young days
when Major Whittle and an evangelist named Leonard
came to our town, I took the step of joining the church
with a group of adolescent friends of my own age. I seemed

---

[1] Exceptions to this rule were my expenses or small honoraria when speaking in colleges, and in latter days the salary I received for lecturing at
two Illinois colleges for a year.

to have a personal, possessive salvation which all unconsciously was selfish and short-circuited. It left out a whole
world of impoverished, suffering humanity for whom I
recognized no responsibility. My religion was conventional,
secondhand, casual, and relatively passive.

Then came the experience at the student conference at
Northfield, when religion became vital and sent me out to
gain others to a way of life and to proclaim a message to
the world. Religion could no longer be solitary; it must be
a *shared* experience. I saw wide areas of the earth in material poverty, millions of human beings lacking education
and knowledge of medical science, living in ignorance,
idolatry, and superstition, with no conception of God as
Father or men as brothers, and I was responsible for
sharing all I had with them. In those days the other half
of the world seemed very far away, and plunging into such
service seemed irrevocable! Yet the appeal was compelling
enough to call fifteen thousand students from North America to plant their lives over six continents, from the poles
to the equator, from Grenfell in Labrador to Zwemer in
the heart of the Moslem world. This missionary crusade
made an immediate challenge to our generation for the
sacrificial and heroic, like the crusades of the Middle Ages,
like the battle charge of Islam, or the Communism-or-
death alternative of Lenin and his revolutionary followers.

When at Northfield I had heard Henry Clay Trumbull,
one of God's most perfect gentlemen, say that some thirty
years previous he had resolved that whenever he met a
man and could choose the subject of conversation that
subject should be Christ and the spiritual life, and that
never in all those years had he met with a single rebuff or

insult, nor in some ten thousand interviews had any man ever resented his kindly approach. Although I never made any such resolution, for many years I followed the practice of speaking to men quite frankly about religion. During the decades I suppose I have spoken individually to several thousand men. I, too, never met with a single rebuff, nor do I recall any man who showed resentment at the conversation—save one. I once made a journey by sea from Calcutta to Madras. When I first boarded the ship I looked across the deck and asked myself who should be the first man tackled. I spotted my man and spoke to him. But the moment I mentioned religion he turned on me furiously and gave me such a broadside that I realized he was suffering from some complex, that there was in him some root of bitterness, probably because of an inner conflict with his own ideals. I made no defense and tried only to keep smiling as Henry Clay Trumbull would have done.

The next day when the man came on deck he apologized for his rudeness but we had another round. On the third day he said that he was sorry I was not continuing on the ship, and I invited him to come ashore with me while the steamer was in port at Madras. There he made one last stand in his defensive fortress and then broke down and confessed his morally rotten life; for he had gone pretty thoroughly to the devil in the tropics "east of Suez." He came out of this morass and went on his way rejoicing, writing back from Canada with gratitude.

On another occasion after a "religious emphasis week" in an eastern college I boarded the Pennsylvania Limited so utterly fagged that I could scarcely see straight or even keep awake. I decided to go into the barber shop to get a long-deferred haircut, and incidentally an even more needed nap. But barbers will talk and this man was no exception. When he told me he had recently been in a train wreck, I replied, half asleep, that so had I. When he said: "I nearly lost my life in that wreck," I answered, dreamily, "So did I." Then I said: "Well, suppose you had lost your life. Were you ready? Are you ready now to cash in on your chips?" "No," he said, "I'm not ready. Far from it." "Well," I replied, "it's quite simple to get ready," and I told him how he could do so. "Oh," he said, "I *know* all about it. I've heard 'em all preach." "Yes," I said, "you *know* all about it. You're so near that all you would have to do would be to say 'Yes' to God, to come clean, turn right about face, and begin a new life here and now."

But this turning about he flatly refused. I left him and started back to my berth, saying: "Remember, if ever you are ready to say 'Yes' to God, you can step across the line into a new life. Good-by." A little later I saw him coming down the aisle looking for me. He said: "Ah, here you are. I've come to say 'Yes.' After you left, God spoke to me and I got right down on my knees in that little barber shop and gave him my life. I've come to thank you for speaking to me."

When the barber got off the train at Chicago he went down to a slum mission and offered his help in the work carried on there. At the other end of his run in New York he joined in the rescue work of the Salvation Army. On his regular runs on that train he began to tackle the unsuspecting men who came into his barber shop. He asked every man if he was prepared *now* to meet his God! At this safe distance we can smile at the thought of a helpless man, his face covered with lather, watching a strange barber grimly sharpening his razor and earnestly asking his victim if was prepared to meet his God, if he was "ready to die *now*"! When I last heard of this barber he was on his way to France in World War I to ask the boys going "over the top" if they were ready.

Just as it was logical for my solitary religion to become a shared religion, by the same process I passed into a *social* interpretation of the gospel. I had specialized in retail sins but knew little about the wholesale brand, about what Professor Ross used to call "sinning by syndicate." The "class struggle" was only a phrase to me, and the "labor problem" an unexplored realm. I believed in the steward-ship of money but had little comprehension of the social force inherent in the growing concentration of wealth. "Socialism" was only a distasteful word to me, and I had never thought seriously of ways in which the people could use government as a powerful instrument for their eco-nomic and social betterment.

Behind the grim Medusa's head of the carnage at the front in World War I, I began gradually to see the symp-toms of a world which at heart is hostile. As an abscess may become the focal point of a diseased and poisoned body, so the war became to me the symbol and evidence of a sick and envenomed social order. Beneath the con-flict I saw a world of perpetual strife between classes, races, and nations. I saw industrial strikes and lockouts between employers and employed, conflict between rich and poor. I saw prejudice and bitterness between peoples East and West, black and white, yellow and brown. I saw that wars were the logical and almost inevitable result of the whole competitive economic system, which is fundamentally a war system and, therefore, ever in unstable equilibrium.

As a hitherto provincial, self-satisfied American I became conscious for the first time that most of the people of the world live in *Asia* and that six of the seven most populous countries are located on that crowded continent. Most of the world is *colored,* and any policy of "white supremacy" is ultimately doomed. Most of the world is *poor.* Per capita income in the United States is fourteen times that of Africa, sixteen times that of the Middle East, over twenty times the average of south Asia, and nearly fifty times the average of southeast Asia and China. Most of the world is *ill fed* and nearly two-thirds of its people go to bed undernourished. Most of the world is *sick* and the majority have no access to scientific medicine or surgery. Most of the world is *illiterate;* the preponderance of the population of Asia and Africa cannot read or write.

Though inevitably bound up with the economic order, conditioned and compromised by it, I came to the conclusion that henceforth I must live a social life, proclaim a social message, and help to organize a socialized society. As I turned to restudy Jesus' way of life, I found his teaching was summed up in the two great commands to love God and one's neighbor as oneself. This philosophy he illustrated by the parable of the Good Samaritan, who went out to bind up bruised and bleeding humanity, and exemplified in his own life by the bold challenging of the social evil of the money-changers in the Temple.

Our task, then, was not only to win or change individuals, all-important as that was, but to build a new social order and to Christianize the whole of life and all its re-

lations, industrial, social, racial, and international. We had
not only to pluck brands from the burning but to put out
the fire. We had not only to relieve poverty and misery but
to remove their causes.

Looking back into recent history I saw that when the
Church confronted the system of slavery it was not enough
for church members to have a "personal religion" or for
the Church to attempt to Christianize all individual slave-
owners and make them benevolent, while converting the
slaves with promises of a future heaven for all slaves. It
was necessary not only to convert individuals but socially
to abolish an inhuman system which was destroying individuals and poisoning both races—white and black,
owners and owned. Only when religion was concerned with
the whole of life, and was not merely a watertight com-
partment of it, could it appeal to all that was deepest and
best in men.

At last this conception began to grip me with the authentic insistence of the earlier missionary crusade. Religion was now not only a solitary personal experience and
a shared experience but a social experience as well. It
began to assume the proportions of a whole message concerned with the whole of life. It seemed to me that men
must be blind if they could not see what a terrible mess we
had made of the world, and they must be worse than
shallow optimists if they believed that a mere repetition
or proclamation of any doctrine, however orthodox, would
make the world right after so many centuries of failure. It
was more than doubtful whether nineteen additional centuries of the customary emphasis of organized religion
would meet the world's increasing tragedy and solve its

problems. Owing partly to the teaching of that true prophet, Walter Rauschenbusch, with thousands of others after the war I began gropingly to realize the social implications of religion.

While I continued to seek to change individuals, to establish right relations between man and God, I began with others of like mind to work to build a new social order based upon the demands of economic justice, a social order that would include clean politics, complete racial brotherhood, and international co-operation toward the goal of abolishing war and substantiating peace.

The proclamation of a new social message involved the exposure of our unjust social order and meant inevitable controversy. Reactionary vested interests have opposed almost every radical new message, whether argued by Socrates, Roger Bacon, Copernicus, Columbus, Galileo, Kepler, Newton, or the army of martyrs. It was under the conviction that I would be embroiled in controversy that I went to Vienna in 1920 to meet John R. Mott, the head of the North America YMCA, and to resign from the Association. I felt I could not continue to ask rich men for their money while, at the same time, I criticized their methods of making that money. I knew that many of the men I had solicited would never tolerate the social gospel I felt impelled to proclaim. My wife and I agreed that we would stand together as we embarked upon this uncharted and hazardous course.

In answer to my proposed resignation, Mott replied that no organization needed a social gospel more than did the YMCA. He asked me not to resign, but when I returned to New York I placed my resignation before the International Committee. They also refused to accept it. I warned them that I was bound to embarrass them personally, for many of them were men of wealth, and that there would be trouble for the Association. And soon there was. Judge Gary took up the cudgels for big business and by implication threatened a boycott of the YMCA by industrial leaders. He demanded my expulsion from the Association; like-minded industrialists from Chicago seconded the demand. The battle was on and life became increasingly exciting, with all the zest of big-game hunting once again. There was plenty of jungle and more than enough game, red in tooth and claw.

In addition to the capitalists who took up the fight on the side of Judge Gary, organizations began to line up. The American Legion repeatedly tried to have my meetings canceled. The commander of the Legion said he would like to see me silenced in peacetime and shot in time of war. The Daughters of the American Revolution, the Better America Federation, and other convinced or professional patrioteers were likewise not failing in their duty to save the country from an individual who, according to them, was being "supported by Moscow gold"; and they were all the more certain of my contamination because I had long advocated the recognition of Soviet Russia by our government. I now had the privilege of having my name appear on the honor rolls of the various black lists.

The stormy encounters, the hecklers, the public denunciations—these were dramatic. But underneath lay deep problems which had to be thought through. I faced the looming alternatives of individualism and collectivism, capitalism and socialism, Fascism and Communism. These systems I had known only traditionally, following them blindly or rejecting them by inherited prejudice. Now I had to study each on its merits and arrive at a critical, and if possible unprejudiced, judgment concerning all of them.

As my work carried me north and south in our own country and east and west across the world among people white and black, yellow and brown, the problem of race obtruded itself and would not be downed. Racial justice, equal education, Oriental immigration, segregation vs. social intercourse, mob violence and lynching, Negro subjection and anti-Semitism—these were all facets of the problem.

The postwar world was a world with much of its faith destroyed. In American colleges and among the youth of other lands I found that the old conventions and standards had been shattered. The same was true for many adults. There was a period approaching moral anarchy with many persons demanding, or quietly taking, the right to have their fling in dissipation, in unlimited sexual experience, sometimes in avowed free love. The situation could not be met merely by laying down the law of an older generation, nor by imposing the authority of traditional religious sanctions, nor by marshaling the conventional proprieties. Youth for the most part cared for none of these criteria of conduct.

And so I had to study the whole problem of the relations of men and women, of sex education, companionate marriage, lawful marriage, divorce, birth control. This appraisal meant reading books in a new field, everything from Havelock Ellis to Margaret Sanger; it meant hundreds of interviews with perplexed youth and listening to the problems of unadjusted married couples. It meant scores of open forums and finally the organization of my own thinking in a book which was published in 1928 under the title *Sex and Youth*.

Naturally these new problems raised fundamental ethical issues. If the old puritanical or conventional moral standards were challenged, or repudiated, or made impotent for many people, what was to become of the ultimate bases of ethical obligation? What was to determine right and wrong? Was the content of the moral code always relative, always changing? If so, were there then any ultimate grounds of moral obligation remaining or any categorical moral imperative left? Could one find reliable ethical standards in a universal human experience interpreted by reason, apart from traditional authority?

Not only the problem of morals but that of religion had to be faced anew. In country after country I found organized religion challenged, or opposed, or persecuted, as in Russia, Turkey, and China. In some lands Christianity was counted the ally of capitalism, imperialism, and militarism. Even more serious was the utter indifference with which it was treated by many. Others held that religion was not only conservative but reactionary and often positively antisocial; that from age to age it had been in alliance with the worst evils of the *status quo,* as in the case of slavery, the war system, and present-day capitalism. Many asked: "Why religion anyway? What function can such an ineffective and reactionary force perform? Is it not a vestigial survival?"

In an age of scientific skepticism, of sophisticated cynicism, disillusionment, or unbelief, in which many had lost any positive theory of existence, could I work out a philosophy of life that could stand in the fierce light which beats upon our time? Could I rationally evolve my own credo, of which I need be no more ashamed than any Communist of his more dogmatic faith? Was there some reason why more millions were following two men than any others who had ever lived—Jesus of Nazareth and Karl Marx? Were their two philosophies mutually exclusive at all points and wholly incompatible in their contrasted solutions of the problems of life? Or was a creative and constructive synthesis possible between a religious point of view and radical social views? If, in an age of revolutionary change and relentless criticism, I could not hope to formulate a fully rounded philosophy of life, could I in the midst of the battle hew out at least a working faith?

At last I arrived at what was for me a whole gospel, both personal and social. I now wanted to challenge men to thought, to decision, to commitment, to action. To my marrow I had always felt constrained to be an evangelist; now I became a social evangelist, elated with the joy of seeing life whole for the first time.

In 1922 I published the first of many pamphlets dealing with social questions: *America; Its Problems and Perils.* In that year I was invited to deliver the Fondren Lectures at Southern Methodist University, and then the Sturtevant Lectures at Allegheny College. In looking over my published volume of these lectures, *Facing the Crisis,* I notice that Part II is devoted to social and industrial questions, with these subheadings: "Outstanding National Problems," "The Race Question," "The Ethics of War," "Industrial Unrest," "Wealth and Poverty," "Collective Bargaining," "The Open and Closed Shop," "The Social Gospel," "The Christian Solution," "Motives and Objectives," "The Faith of a Modern Christian."

In 1922 and 1923 I made a trip around the world to study the industrial situation and conditions of labor in China, Japan, India, the Far East, Germany, France, Great Britain, and Russia. Having failed, in spite of consistent effort, to secure an industrial expert to work with me, I had to make the study alone.

In the whole industrial world I found the worst conditions in China. There, in 1922, the twelve-hour day prevailed in modern factories, while in primitive Chinese industries the workday ranged from twelve to sixteen, and in some cases even eighteen hours, seven days a week. Children from six to twelve years of age were working for wages of three to twelve cents a day. Housing conditions were unspeakable. In Shanghai I found one broad shelf serving as a "home" for six men, one of whom was dying of tuberculosis, coughing night and day. Their collective rent was $1.15 per month. Conditions were far worse than they had been at the time of the industrial revolution in England.

From each country I sent home report letters through my private secretary, whose support was provided by Madam McCormick. When I reached London I went to hear my friend, Maude Royden, preach, and after the service was invited by her to a late supper with John D. Rockefeller, Jr. Mr. Rockefeller thanked me for my recent report letters and said he had been reading them to his father and to his sons. He invited me to dine with his family and asked me to tell them about "those boys in China, Japan, and India." To help meet the abysmal needs of China he gave me $25,000 a year for three years, the money to be administered by the China Council of Churches, the YMCA, and the YWCA. It was hoped that this experiment in China would eventually show the way to change the inferno in which most of the cheap labor in Asia were living. There were 570,000,000 of them—more than twice the number of people employed in Europe and America combined.

At the end of the tour, in the library of the International Labor Organization at Geneva, I wrote *The New World of Labor*. In that book I made this challenge:

History repeats itself, from the strike of the oppressed Hebrew bricklayers in Egypt to the volcanic upheaval in autocratic Czarist Russia. And yet in every age, learning nothing and forgetting nothing, a Bourbon class arises in industrial, political or religious life, claiming a special privilege which in the nature of the case can only be enjoyed by a small minority, at the expense of the rights of the vast majority. And in every age, just because it is human and cannot deny its God-given irrepressible instincts, that majority rises, organizes and claims its rights, peaceably if it be under a rule of liberty, violently if it be under a system of repression. Man has at last won liberty of conscience in the religious sphere, the ballot and some measure of democracy in the political sphere; he has not yet won industrial democracy or justice in his economic life.

In addition to writing and speaking, I gave my support to organizations working for social change in ways that seemed sound and wise to me. I helped to found the Fellowship for a Christian Social Order and was a member of the early group out of which came the Fellowship of Socialist Christians. I voted for Norman Thomas. And I had the privilege of paying Reinhold Niebuhr's salary during his first years at Union.

As truly as my early personal gospel had driven me to the ends of the earth with its "woe is me if I preach not," so now the preaching of this new whole gospel meant even greater adventure. I soon found that it called for a fight to the finish, and that I loved it.

Chapter 7

❦

THE SEMINARS IN EUROPE

In the summer of 1920 my new-found urge to explore social situations and seek solutions for social problems led me to study abroad as well as at home. With the help of Jimmie Mallon, beloved Warden of Toynbee Hall, I made a study of the British labor movement, attended the Trades Union Congress, met Ramsay MacDonald, Arthur Henderson, and other labor leaders. Suddenly the idea flashed into my mind, and was cordially approved by Dr. Mallon; Why not bring over annually from the United States a selected group of educators and lecturers for this illuminating and enriching experience? They could meet the leaders of all political parties and other outstanding men throughout Europe and then return to America to speak and write about their findings. Perhaps this exchange of ideas which the meetings would provide would be one avenue to international understanding and peace. And so in 1921 began the annual pilgrimage which came to be known as the American Seminar. It continued for nearly two decades, until 1939, when World War II made its continuance impossible. In 1950, at the suggestion of British leaders who hoped to strengthen the ties between Britain and America, it was reorganized as the Sherwood

Eddy Seminar and has since conducted a party of some fifty lecturers, educators, and ministers through the principal countries of Europe each summer.

The first party included, among others, Bishop Charles D. Williams of Detroit, Bromley Oxnam, Governor William E. Sweet of Colorado, Fletcher Brockman, Henry P. Van Dusen, Paul Blanshard, Jerome Davis, Sidney Gamble, Arthur Holt, George Stewart, Alva W. Taylor, Kirby Page, Cameron Hall, and Ben Cherrington. The first speaker to address our group at Toynbee Hall, where the London sessions were held, was Ramsay MacDonald, speaking on the coal strike. Before our visit had ended we had listened to and engaged in discussion with R. H. Tawney, Sidney Webb, G. D. H. Cole, George Lansbury, Margaret Bondfield, Philip Kerr (later Lord Lothian), Seebohm Roundtree, Harold Laski, W. E. Orchard, A. E. Garvie, Bishop Temple, Hugh Dalton, Philip Snowden, Robert Smillie, J. A. Hobson, and Arthur Greenwood. Lord Robert Cecil addressed us at the League of Nations Union House. Lady Astor gave us a reception at her home, a courtesy which she repeated almost annually, and Ramsay MacDonald and Arthur Henderson invited us to tea on the terrace of the House of Commons. Similar invitations were extended year after year.

Our first program on the Continent laid foundations for future years. In Germany we were entertained by former Chancellor Michaelis, who later visited me in America. In Berlin we had a memorable interview with Walter Rathenau, Minister of Reparations and one of the most impressive men I ever met. One of our "finds" was Dr. Arnold Wolfers, who arranged many of our subsequent

programs in Berlin, before coming to Yale. A small group
of us toured for three hundred miles through Upper
Silesia in a car provided by the German Foreign Office,
and saw conditions under Allied armed occupation, pend-
ing the decision of the League of Nations as to whether
Upper Silesia should be awarded to Germany or to
Poland.

One year, at the close of our stay in Berlin, we had the
privilege of meeting Einstein. We motored out for an hour
and he came in from the country to meet us for tea. He
presented a striking personality—a childlike spirit with a
giant brain. With long white hair, full oval face, large
luminous eyes, he was modest, humble, kindly, humorous,
and above all human. In the course of the conversation he
said: "My pacifism is an immediate feeling. Mass murder
and the destruction of human life is to me horrible, impossible. I am glad to see in the world today a rising tide
of peace, a growing sentiment for it. But it is not enough
as yet to avert a sudden catastrophe of war." How true his
words proved to be! And that day little did he foresee the
ghastly tyranny of Hitler.

In 1923 the third seminar group included Reinhold
Niebuhr, Bishop William Scarlett, James H. Causey, E. E.
Barnett, Kirby Page, W. O. Mendenhall, and some fifty
members. Among others we were addressed by Lloyd
George, Lord Haldane, Lord Milner, Bernard Shaw, Gil-
bert Murray, Maude Royden, and H. G. Wells. The successive Archbishops of Canterbury met with us annually:
Lord Davidson, and later Cosmo Lang, William Temple,
and Geoffrey Fisher.

In the Ruhr in 1923, then under French armed occupation, I saw the making of the Second World War and wrote home this warning:

I believe the present policy of the French Government is both futile and fatal and will ultimately drag the world into war as surely as did the events of 1870 and 1914. I came into the Ruhr skeptical, doubting stories that I had heard, but after talking with scores of witnesses and after myself witnessing robberies and acts of violence, I am forced to say soberly that for shooting, cruelty, injustice, robberies of banks and of private individuals, I have seen nothing equal to this French occupation of the Ruhr since I left the province of the bandits in Honan, China. In China these barbarisms were committed by bandits in defiance of the Government. In the Ruhr they are perpetrated by the Government of a nation that boasts of "liberty, equality and fraternity."

I took photographs of French soldiers and their officers robbing German banks, and sometimes saw them taking money from pedestrians on the street. A member of our Seminar, James Causey, a businessman of Denver and later on Wall Street, was so moved at the sight of the sufferings of the Germans in the Ruhr that he proposed that he and I raise a fund of $500,000 to keep trainloads of food flowing into the distressed area by a system of revolving credits. Though Causey did more than nine-tenths of the work, I helped him raise this fund, chiefly from the bankers in Berlin, London, and New York and from Americans of German ancestry throughout the United States. We fed the Ruhr during the entire French occupation. Then, to our surprise, the Germans paid back the entire sum of $500,000 and gave us each year some token of their gratitude at luncheons or teas given by the *Junkers,* the Berlin Chamber of Commerce, or the Chancellor.

Each year during a week in Berlin we met the successive

German leaders, among them the first President of the Weimar Republic, the labor leader Ebert, and the second President, the aged General von Hindenburg. On his desk was his motto, "Watch and pray," and to the last the old man always spoke to us of peace. Hitler finally brushed him aside and went out to conquer the world. I met the successive Chancellors from Michaelis and Luther to Wirth, Bruning, and later von Papen. I once asked von Papen how he dared allow Hitler to become Chancellor. His proud reply implied that he had only given Hitler three places on the cabinet, while he himself controlled von Hindenburg with the army and the police; yet von Papen barely escaped with his life in Hitler's first "blood bath" purge when he killed several hundred of his enemies in one day, June 30, 1934.

I saw Hitler and heard him make that awful speech in which he boasted of killing his enemies. We drove in our automobile through miles of soldiers and police who lined the streets, passed the Reichstag that the Nazis had already burned, up to the Kroll Opera House where Hitler was to speak. I have the photograph before me of Hitler alighting from his car to make that speech. I stood within five feet of him and the back of my head appears in the photograph, but my hand is not raised in a "Heil Hitler" salute. That year I felt that the crisis in Germany made impossible mere conventional politeness. I felt constrained to ask the Nazis in my address in the House of the Press whether, as in 1914, they were dragging us up to the precipice of another world war. I asked them whether they were giving justice to all their people or only to favored Aryans and Nordics. Were they giving or denying justice to the Jews, to socialists, to pacifists and other minorities? I asked if they had not denied all liberty of speech, of the press, of association and assembly to their people. We had just left England where the Archbishop of Canterbury had taken the chair at a meeting of protest against Germany's medieval persecution of the Jews and other minorities. I told them that we had not found a word reporting this meeting in their controlled press. I held up to the gathering a textbook of the Nazi schools, one of a series instilling hatred of the Jewish race, which out of all proportion to its numbers had furnished so many great leaders in Germany for the last two hundred years, from the time of Moses Mendelssohn to Einstein. After my attack on Naziism, the account of which was published the next day in the *London Times,* the *New York Times,* and the Associated Press from coast to coast, I never left the hotel alone.

Each year in Berlin we met Dr. Schacht as he spoke to our Seminar in his Reichsbank. I remember how his face glowed with enthusiasm the first time he described Hitler to me as a selfless patriot who "neither smoked, nor drank nor had any interest in women"—in contrast to Mussolini. We also met Reichsbischof Muller who told us his plan for a pure Nordic church freed from Jews—and apparently from Christ—with the "good old German God," the war god Jahweh, who now resembled the pagan Thor and Wodin. In successive years we saw four swift kaleidoscopic changes in Germany under the Kaiser, the Weimar Republic, Hitler's dictatorship, and then after World War II the divided Berlin of East and West Germany.

In Geneva the Seminar studied the League of Nations at its headquarters, holding an annual conference there;

and in Paris we were addressed by various leaders. One section of our Seminar regularly visited Italy. One year under the direction of Charles P. Taft the members had the unusual experience of meeting Pope Pius XI, Mussolini, Cardinal Pacelli, who later became Pope Pius XII, and Cardinal Spellman—all in one day.

With the Seminar and on personal trips I came to know well both Czarist and Soviet Russia, which I visited fifteen times; twice under the Czars, in 1910 and 1912; thirteen times under the Soviet regime, in 1923, 1926, 1929, and then annually through 1939. Under the Czars, the Russian nobility to the very end dined and danced and caroused over the exploited bodies of the people. A shot in far-off Serajevo brought about the precipitous mobilization of the Russian imperial army, which proved to be the match that ignited World War I. Then under the weight of corruption and the waging of war on a colossal scale came the collapse of the old Czarist system followed by the Kerensky revolution and later, on November 7, 1917, by the seizure of power by Lenin and Trotsky.

Once more I was almost on the ground floor of revolution, arriving six years after Bolshevism had achieved power, two years following the adoption of the New Economic Policy, and only a year after the terrible famine which affected forty million people. When I arrived in 1923, few foreign visitors were being admitted to Russia. Memories of civil war were still vivid, and only three years before had the Allied armies of occupation withdrawn, including the armed forces of the United States in Siberia. I found the people just emerging from the abyss of misery. They had suffered from World War I, two revolutions, civil war between the Red and White armies, invasion by fourteen foreign armies fighting at one time on a dozen fronts, and a world blockade to starve Russia. Some ten million people had perished. Industrial production had fallen to 17 per cent of the Czarist maximum. The government had had to face the sabotage and opposition of the old bureaucracy and the bourgeois class but somehow had managed to survive. In 1923 minimum wages were twenty-five cents per day. With the Soviet's depreciated and inflated currency I paid a fortune of 65 million rubles for a pair of shoelaces, 96 million rubles for half a large loaf of bread, and 26 million rubles for a ride on a streetcar.

I did not go to Russia because I had any fondness for Communism but because, from the beginning, the experiment there seemed to be both a warning and a challenge to us. I had great eagerness to understand what was going on. Not until 1926 was I able to make arrangements for the first visit of the American Seminar, composed of twenty-four educators, editors, religious leaders, social workers, and businessmen. Four members of our group spoke Russian. Among the members of our party were Charles Clayton Morrison, Chester Rowell, Jerome Davis, William H. Danforth, Louise Gates, William Scarlett, Tully Knoles, Kirby Page, Fred W. Ramsey, Mrs. Ralph Adams Cram, Cameron Hall, Matthew Spinka, and Sidney Gamble.

We had talks with about thirty political leaders, including Chicherin, Minister of Foreign Affairs, and Lunacharsky, Minister of Education. Jerome Davis, who spoke Russian, obtained an interview with Stalin. We visited all possible places of importance, including the historic Kremlin and the Czar's palaces. We were amazed when we were permitted to view the crown jewels of the Czar and saw spread before us all this beauty and untold wealth. We saw factories, schools, prisons, museums, art galleries, and the institutions of social education and service for workers and peasants.

In the early years of Communism, before Stalin had killed or imprisoned his enemies, there were things good and bad side by side in Russia, and evidences of the early idealism embodied in the first Russian constitution could be found.

One of their fine experiments which I frequently visited was a model Reclamation Colony at Bolshevo in the beautiful pine woods two hours out of Moscow. It was one of fifty such model penal colonies, founded on the theory that environment shapes the organism; in place of the popular slogan "You can never change human nature," Russian penalists held with Marx that "the whole of history is nothing but the progressive transformation of human nature." In the light of the riots and violence in our own unsatisfactory penal system I was impressed by the early Soviet system, before Stalin swept it all away with his merciless police state.

Of two thousand inmates at Bolshevo most were once hardened young thieves or criminals who had been convicted several times. All were placed on their honor under a voluntary system of self-government. There were no prison bars, not even a barbed-wire fence around the colony, and anyone could leave if he wished. I found a large farm, trade schools, machine shops, and manufacturing departments where each inmate could choose his own trade. The institution seemed almost like an American college, for over five hundred belonged to interest groups and circles, with five bands and orchestras, a glee club, a dramatic club, sports clubs, athletic teams, and numerous entertainments. Anyone could marry and settle down if he obtained the consent of the convicts' own elected Commission. A town and community had been built up around the colony where men could settle permanently if they chose, at the expiration of their indeterminate sentences.

One year we arrived at the colony when all of the five superintendents and overseers had been unexpectedly summoned to a conference in Moscow. Our Seminar party of fifty had the whole day among the inmates to do what we liked; we were free to question them individually or in groups. We heard the orchestra practicing Beethoven's Fifth Symphony, we visited the homes, asked various men what they had learned from their life of crime or from their stay in the institution. Many testified that they were changed men. At the end of the day a member of our group, a young instructor at Cornell, said he felt as if he had been worshiping in some great cathedral.

A second illustration of early Soviet idealism I discovered when we called upon Prince Ossinsky, thousands of acres of whose former princely estate we had seen. He was glad that it was then all in the hands of the former peasant serfs. As "the Henry Ford of Russia," he was responsible for manufacturing all the automobiles, trucks, and tractors for the whole USSR. He confirmed the fact that he, with all other members of the Communist party, was then limiting himself to the "party maximum" of five dollars a day for personal support. I suggested that Henry Ford, who was reported to have made a profit in a recent year of some eighty million dollars, or over $200,000 a day, would never be satisfied with five dollars a day, which would be less than any day laborer in his factory was paid. Ossinsky smiled and said: "I have a comfortable home and all my personal needs are supplied. Think! If we could build, not just a new Russia, but *a new world,* what would money matter? Would it make any difference whether I received five or two hundred thousand dollars a day?"

The thought was startling. It was evident that he really believed, with other idealists in the early revolution, that they were building a veritable new world! Later in the purges Stalin had Ossinsky shot with thousands of others whom he suspected of agreement with Trotsky or who differed from him on the right or on the left. All the other members of Lenin's first Politbureau and most of the heroic "old Bolsheviks" who had risked their lives for the revolution were "liquidated" by Stalin until the early idealism of the movement was destroyed. Yet so secretly were most of these purges conducted—men simply disappeared at midnight from their homes—that years afterward many of the youth of Russia still believed they alone could build a new world and were prepared to sacrifice life itself to that great end.

One of the high lights of our visit to Russia in 1926 was a session when we frankly voiced to a group of Russian leaders our major criticisms of what we had seen and heard in the Soviet Union. Rudziatak, then head of the railways and a member of the Political Bureau, had told us with keen disappointment of an American businessman who had appeared to be friendly to them while selling his goods who had bitterly criticized their whole regime after he returned to America. It suddenly occurred to me that these leaders might say the same of our entire party, for we were most certainly going to criticize them upon our return to our own country. Accordingly we had an interview with Trotsky's sister, Madam Kameneva, then the head of the Cultural Relations Society, responsible for all foreigners in Russia. I suggested, and she cordially agreed, that we should meet the Soviet leaders for a conference to tell them exactly what we thought of their system. We would state our every criticism or indictment of it, then give them an opportunity to reply and state their side of the case.

So the meeting was arranged. Our party of twenty-four Americans held a caucus to discuss what appeared to us to be the chief evils or defects in the Soviet system. Four of our number were chosen to present the four principal indictments. These were handed in writing in advance to the Soviet leaders, and four of their number were chosen to present their point of view. The evils we singled out were: their totalitarian dictatorship with its severe abridgment of liberty; their policy of world revolution by violence; their atheistic opposition to religion; and their ruthless international relationships, which did not encourage co-operation, recognition, loans, concessions, or trade. For four hours we attacked them unsparingly upon these four vulnerable points, and listened to their speakers. Never in any other country or upon any other occasion have I been more brutally frank, more merciless in criticism. Our arguments were received and replied to in the finest spirit. It was one of the most interesting and enlightening discussions I have ever known. The attitude of the Kremlin twenty years ago was very different from what it is today.

And out of this came another significant experience. I had pointed out to the Soviet leaders that in three cities of Russia, under the unspeakable Czarist regime in 1912, I had been able to give lectures and conduct religious meetings for students. Why then was I not free to do so under the present regime? Why was this the only government on earth which laid claim to being civilized, which did not permit public meetings or lectures for students upon the subject of religion? When the editor of *The Godless* magazine rose to reply, he stated that the Soviet constitution, which guaranteed liberty of conscience, did not prohibit our holding such meetings. Whereupon I challenged him to a debate the following Sunday on the subject of religion: "Theism versus Atheism, Christianity versus Communism." He immediately accepted the challenge and we agreed upon the terms of the debate. There were to be four speakers: two Christians—a Russian friend and myself—and two Communists. Each speaker was to be allowed an hour, with questions following. Seats were to be sold and the proceeds were to go to an orphanage.

A large hall was obtained in the city, a notice was put in the papers, and within forty-eight hours every seat was sold. Those of us who were upholding religion expected to meet an audience of atheists and probably go down to a forensic defeat, but in so doing we hoped to open a little wider the door of tolerance and religious liberty. To my surprise, about one-third of the audience were Christians who boldly heckled the Communist speakers, as the atheists heckled me and the Russian Christian who spoke. Some two hundred written questions were handed up to be answered. After five hours the meeting disbanded.

No such discussion with leaders and no debates were permitted three years later or ever again. By that time Russia was in the midst of a prolonged battle between the forces of religion and antireligion. In many homes I saw the icons supplanted by pictures of Lenin. In others the icon was in one corner and a picture of Lenin in the other, sometimes signifying a divided allegiance, either between husband and wife or between parents and children or in the heart of the same person. I witnessed three most aggressive drives against religion conducted by the Militant Godless Society.

In a letter to my old friend Raymond Robins, dated August 17, 1929, I expressed my deep concern over the intensifying terror and the religious persecution:

Several thousand have been exiled under the terror, and several thousand more under religious persecution. The Government is quite willing to allow the droning services in the Orthodox Church, though an increasing number of churches are being closed, but the moment any man, or group, or church is obviously modern or scientific or successful, the moment they stand for unity or cooperation or internationalism, they must be quickly, and if possible quietly suppressed. A Christian Student Movement is allowed in every civilized country in the world except Soviet Russia. Here it has been completely crushed out. This is the only country on earth where I would not dare meet three students in a room to talk about religion. If it were known, it would mean immediate exile for them, and I would never again be allowed to return here.

Twice I talked with Krassikov, the Attorney General of the Soviet Union, about the persecution of religion, but received from him no satisfaction whatever. I had in my pocket the handkerchief of the girl who was my interpreter, red with her blood. She had been cruelly struck by a raging atheist ex-priest in the torture chambers of the GPU until her lungs had bled freely. I stated my protest in writing against the whole totalitarian system and handed it to Krassikov, but later the Attorney General himself was shot by order of Stalin in one of the three great purges.

Yaroslavsky, president of the Union of Militant Godless and a member with Stalin of the Political Bureau, after fifteen years of zealous antireligious activity assisted by lavish government spending admitted frankly to our Seminar party and repeated in his speech reported in the *Bezbojnik* of April 17, 1933, that they had not been able to uproot religion in Russia: "At the present moment the Union of Militant Godless counts five and a half million members. . . . In the Trade Unions over 40 per cent are godless . . . and there are not less than 10 million godless among the tens of millions on the collective farms." But again he said: "If we are to estimate the entire number of believers [in religion] in our country at 100 millions, and this means more than half of the entire population, I would say not less than half the total number of children are believers." The Soviets of course succeeded in winning the majority of the children in their materialistic system of education. Later, however, when Stalin recognized the church and tried to use it as his tool, his very approval effected an even greater threat to religion.

After writing *The Challenge of Russia* in 1930, and *Russia Today* in 1934, I continued in a report letter: "I am not, I never could be, a Communist. Because of the persistent evils in the system, even more evident today than they were two decades ago, that position is for me a moral impossibility. I could never accept such a denial of political and civil liberties. I could never stand for the violence of the continuing revolution which never ends till the last enemy has been destroyed. And I could never accept, nor defend, the harsh dogmatism, the blatant atheism and the hundred per cent perfectionism or conformism which the loyal Communist has to profess."

As I reflect on the visits of the American Seminar to Russia, I am amazed that we could go back regularly year after year and were allowed so much freedom. Every member of the Seminar knew that he was free to speak his mind when he returned to the United States, and to write as he saw fit. Personally, I never felt any restraint in voicing my convictions about the situation in Russia. I went all over Russia, often without any guide, spy, or official and was allowed great liberty. I sought eagerly to see every possible value and any possible lesson that America might learn from Russia. However, I am compelled to record the growing evils that began to menace Russia and the world under Stalin.

Despite the sonorous wording of their successive constitutions, I saw the gradual hardening of the police state in Russia where today no man is free. I saw the Soviet Union pass through three awful purges. Then I saw the chief purgers themselves eliminated. There was first the slimy Yagoda who had apparently poisoned Maxim Gorki and carried out Stalin's orders to murder his fellow members of the triumvirate, Kamenev and Zinoviev. Then followed the fanatic Yezhov, his successor as grand inquisitor until he was liquidated.

I saw the official atheism of the Soviet system furnish the logical foundation for immorality and amorality. Then I saw in the distance some of the first of their slave labor camps, which I was never allowed to visit. My friend and fellow engineer H. K. spent two years as a prisoner in these awful camps and then in my office dictated to my secretary an account of his whole experience. He was later murdered by the Communists in Korea because he knew too much.

I saw the whole Soviet Union sink to the level of a slave state, where all, consciously or unconsciously, are prisoners; where no scientist, no musician is free. No theater, no motion picture, no actor, no producer, no writer is free in Russia today. Finally, I saw this degraded slave state of Stalinism embark on its period of world conquest by three methods: by propaganda, such as that concerning "hated American imperialism conquering Korea by germ warfare"; by revolution from within a country, when it becomes rotten-ripe with injustice, as in China; and by invasion, as on June 25, 1950, when the North Koreans, armed with Russian tanks, planes, and armor launched their aggressive war of conquest. By these three methods the Soviet Union now controls about a third of the world and is arming and increasing productive capacity to be able to advance upon the other two-thirds.

What is Russian Communism? Trying to understand and then oppose Soviet Russia I came gradually to realize that basically Russian Communism consists of three elements: It is an economic theory of Karl Marx; it is a power system for world conquest inherited from the imperialistic Czars; but, deepest of all, it is a passionate, fanatical, sacrificial faith, as much as Islam ever was.

Better than statistics, an illustration will show what I mean by Communism's being a religion. On an early visit to the Soviet Union I sat between two young men upon a park bench. Upon my asking how many hours a day in unpaid labor each was working for his Communist cause, one replied three and the other four hours a day. My guide Ellen, a student in the University of Moscow, was working five hours a day, outside her studies. In five languages, she was corresponding with the youth leaders of Europe and America, not of course to Christianize but to communize them. I tried to think of any student in our colleges, or youth in our churches, who was working as effectively and sacrificially as were these young people, whether for America, or for "free enterprise," or for the Church, or for Christianity, for God or man, but I could think of none.

On each visit to Russia, when in Moscow I used to go to Lenin's tomb at five o'clock in the afternoon to take my place in the waiting queue of several thousand young people. When the doors opened I watched them file round the embalmed body of Lenin, every eye fastened upon the face of a man who they believed had lived for his cause for twenty years, in poverty, prison, or exile. A man who, when he held the wealth of Czarist Russia in his hand, had cheerfully lived on two dollars a day in utter simplicity. I watched this silent, almost worshiping, line of youth as they seemed to be trying to fan to flame the flickering spark of devotion in their own hearts. They seemed to be resolving that they, too, would be willing for twenty years, or for a lifetime, in poverty, prison, or exile, to live and die for the cause to which Lenin had given his life.

Personally I do not follow a dead atheist, but a living God and One whose call was sterner far than Lenin's: "He that forsaketh not all that he hath, cannot be my disciple." "If any man will come after me, let him deny himself, and take up his cross and follow me." I follow a religion that repeatedly has its days of heroic sacrifice, that has shown again and again that it has within itself the power of renewal, revival, and reformation. When Christianity won the Roman Empire, "Christians had to outlive the pagans, to outthink them, to out-die them." Today even if we can outfight the Communists on the battlefield, shall we, or our youth, be able to outlive them in sacrifice, to outthink them, to out-die them? I believe that Communism challenges us at this moment not only as an economic theory and a power system of world conquest but most of all as a sacrificial religion. Whatever the evils in the Soviet system—greater far than our own— I believe that Russia dares us to put our house in order nationally, and our lives in order individually, and that we are not yet adequately meeting that challenge.

My trips into Europe took me several times into Czechoslovakia. It was my privilege to be in that country in 1920 during the first thrilling days of the new republic, and to have warm personal contacts with President Masaryk. This son of a coachman, serving as a blacksmith boy, went on to become professor of philosophy at Vienna and at Prague. During the war he conducted a campaign for the freedom of his people from the Hapsburgs. In Switzerland, France, England, Italy, Russia, and America he sought support; in Pittsburgh he prepared the constitution for the new republic; and in 1917 it was adopted by Czechs in Philadelphia beneath our old Liberty Bell. In 1918 the republic was proclaimed in Prague and was confirmed by the Treaty of Versailles in 1920.

High over Prague stood the great castle, then the residence of President Masaryk, probably at that time the most learned and democratic ruler in the world. I was with him in his study looking over those 10,000 volumes in his library, where he worked in four languages. I examined some of the score of books which he himself had written, one of which, *The Spirit of Russia*, he gave me. I was deeply impressed with the character of the President as a great yet humble man who had suffered much for liberty and truth.

In 1938 I was back in Czechoslovakia just a few days before the betrayal of that republic at Munich. I met some of the Czechoslovakians who had attended the first student conference eighteen years previously and who had remained firm in their faith. In a talk with President Beneš, I reminded him that years earlier I had spoken with him and the aged President Masaryk about the Sudeten problem of the German and other minorities, though I little dreamed that day what was ahead: subjugation by Hitler, decimation through massacre, freedom again for a brief moment, then Communist seizure of power and a harsh dictatorship.

President Masaryk at the age of seventy-seven, gifted for a moment as a religious seer or prophet, had foreseen such a tragedy. In an interview with Heintz Leipmann, international journalist and novelist, President Masaryk had said prophetically: "Each time in our long history that our country has been destroyed, we have built up a new and better one; each time our constitution became more liberal than the last had been. *Maybe my country will have to go through one more ordeal*—maybe it will have to be destroyed once more, to be built up as the real, the definite, the eternal democracy."

I visited Czechoslovakia finally in 1947. The speaker of the House of the Czech Parliament left his seat, called another to take his place, and took me up to the gallery where he pointed down to the members of the Parliament voting by parties. He showed me that the Communists then held about two-fifths of the seats on the left. If they could have captured over 50 per cent of the seats they would have seized power and established a dictatorship. Instead, after the excesses, crimes, and purges in Stalin's Russia the Communists were losing seats. Hence suddenly, on orders from Moscow, the Communist party set up their machine guns in the streets of Prague and by a coup seized power and established their ruthless dictatorship. Later Stalin, suspicious and jealous of the leaders in all the satellite states, began to put some of their leaders to death.

Czechoslovakia, once the most glorious democratic republic in continental Europe, has indeed been crucified once again, as it was under the crusade called by the Pope against Protestant Bohemia in 1620, as it was under the iron heel of the Hapsburgs for three centuries thereafter, as it was by the cruelty of Hitler, and last of all under Stalin and the Politbureau of the Kremlin. But since

God is still in his heaven, I believe this former democratic republic will yet realize a more complete democracy in "liberty and justice for all."

On my last visit, on July 4, 1947, at Ambassador Steinhart's garden party in Prague I again saw my friend the greathearted Jan Masaryk, son of the former President and now the Foreign Minister. I told him our State Department was particularly anxious to have Czechoslovakia enjoy all the help of the Marshall Plan. He said he was more anxious for that help than we were, but that he had been summoned by Stalin and Molotov to come to Moscow the next day to receive their orders. I asked him if he would tell me frankly their answer when he returned from Moscow. He said: "I like you, and I will tell you frankly after I return." A week later as I was preparing to leave Czechoslovakia by plane, I received a phone call from Jan Masaryk. I raced up to the hilltop to his palace and finally found him heartsick in bed, utterly discouraged. He told me Czechoslovakia was no longer free; she was not to be allowed to enter the Marshall Plan and he must get strength to dress to go over and inform President Beneš of the bad news. It was, apparently, in that very room that he met his death shortly after, when the Communists killed him and threw his body out of the window to make it appear that he had committed suicide.

When our American Seminar was resumed after World War II, Russia had closed its doors behind the iron curtain but Yugoslavia had opened hers wide. In 1952 Marshal Tito met the Seminar in a frank interview, as he has every year since, and answered our questions for an hour and a half. When I asked him if we might interview Archbishop Stepinac, just released from prison after serving five of his sixteen years, he cordially consented. We found the Archbishop a gaunt, ascetic peasant-born primate of his country's seven million Roman Catholics. The division between the Roman and Orthodox Catholic churches began nine centuries ago with the schism of 1054, when Catholic popes and Orthodox patriarchs excommunicated each other. Nearly nine hundred years later Hitler invaded the country and set up his stooges— Pavelic as head of the state. Stepinac was head of the Church; both were Roman Catholics. It looked as if the old schism might be wiped out and as if Yugoslavia would emerge a strong totalitarian state with the supremacy of the Roman Catholic Church restored.

Toward this end three Orthodox bishops were murdered, 240,000 Orthodox Serbs under forced mass conversion accepted Roman Catholicism, armed Fascist bands of Ustashi, often led by Catholic priests, committed atrocities, and 800,000 Orthodox Christians perished in the war or by atrocities. Archbishop Stepinac was shocked at these unchristian practices and on November 20, 1941, sent *privately* a letter of protest to Pavelic, mentioning villages where "all were killed like beasts." *Publicly,* however, Stepinac supported Pavelic, never condemned his murdering Ustashi priests, and the atrocities continued. When Hitler's troops were defeated and driven out by Marshal Tito's growing guerrilla army, Stepinac took over the crumbling Fascist state.

After World War II, Marshal Tito, wishing no conflict with powerful Rome, laid the mass of evidence of Stepi-

nac's guilt before Rome's representative, Bishop Hurley of
St. Augustine, Florida, asking to have the Archbishop
withdrawn from Yugoslavia. Rome, however, wished
Stepinac to stay as their martyr saint and hero where
St. Jerome (340–420 A.D.) had lived. Stepinac was tried
by the government and on October 4, 1946, made an im-
passioned defense of himself but no refutation of the government's charges. Stepinac's private protest against the
atrocities stands in amelioration of his personal guilt, but
it casts a heavier shadow upon Rome, which had blessed
Pavelic for his zeal as a "practicing Catholic."

When Marshal Tito emerged as his country's hero and
first President, Stalin was bitterly jealous and demanded
that he come to Moscow and abjectly confess his sins. Tito
refused, and published the whole correspondence; his
country overwhelmingly stood by him. Tito now stands
as Russia's most pronounced and bitter threat, especially
since he cemented a close alliance with the fierce-fighting
Turks and Greeks upon Russia's border. He has been
enthusiastically received in Britain by Churchill and the
British people. Doubtless I am prejudiced, but however
great our differences I count Tito a personal friend and
with real affection and confidence watch him working out
his country's destiny.

Chapter 8

BUILDING A NEW AMERICA

When I retired from the Young Men's Christian Association at the age of sixty, I was given a farewell banquet by friends in New York, on January 27, 1931. Addresses were given by Alfred E. Marling, John R. Mott, and Raymond Robins. I was surrounded by old and dear friends, and we all caught the spirit of the festive occasion. Much hilarity was engendered by the brilliant chairman Alfred Marling's attempt to "rate" my traits of character. On the scale of 100 I was given only 48 for modesty, for "shrinking from giving my opinions"; 70 for a sense of humor, which I thought was much too low; companionableness, from 78 to 100 depending upon my degree of preoccupation; 88 for wisdom. But some marks were much higher, 110 for cocksureness, and 116 for nerve!

When I was called upon to speak, I felt that I must lay aside the levity long enough to give a frank statement about some of my deep convictions and concerning my work in the future, so I said: "As I sat on that little hilltop behind the town of Nazareth last year, I read through the Sermon on the Mount and the whole record of Jesus' life. It seemed to me that I could summarize it all in the one word *love*; personal, as self-realization through self-sacrifice, the recognition of the value of personality in the abundant life for each ; and social, love realized in the full sharing of life with all."

I pointed out that this conviction meant several things for me: basic economic justice, brotherhood and fellowship in race relations, clean politics, right international relations, the abolition of war, right relations between men and women, the rediscovery of the religion of Jesus, and the gaining of spiritual dynamic. On the question of politics, I said at that time:

I am not a Communist; I am not a Capitalist; I am a Socialist. I voted for Norman Thomas at the last election and for La Follette at the election before that. My friends, we have got to Christianize our social order. It is not enough to say that Christianity has never been tried. If it has not, why not? If we will not Christianize this social order, there are those who will seek to communize it. We have the remedy if we will apply it and I believe we can apply it. We have to transform life, to make Christlike men and women in a Christlike society, by the intelligent application of love in every relationship of life. What a time to be living!

After retirement I was free from all organizational responsibility, but I continued the work of personal and social evangelism in the colleges, at youth gatherings, and in the churches. I devoted my energies to challenging individuals to give their total allegiance to Christ and to his cause, but I was equally fervent in my plea that we should become consecrated workers in the task of Christianizing the social order. For the next two decades from the platform, in the pulpit, in articles and pamphlets and books, I brought a continuing indictment against our present social order and entreated men to help build a Christian society.

As I survey past history I think I can see that nations pass through various stages in their economic progress. From slavery, to feudalism, to capitalism; then to some form of controlled or regulated capitalism, and finally to the socialized planned economy of a welfare state. Each stage is fiercely defended by its beneficiaries, who condemn the threat of the impending new order. Reactionary neo-Fascists today assure us that "the welfare state is halfway to socialism, socialism is halfway to Communism, and Communism more than halfway to hell."

Many point to America as the shining example of the success of capitalism, imagining that all the world could be prosperous if only they had our "free enterprise," but to me our situation seems wholly unique. Rather than saying that capitalism made America great, it would be truer to say that America made capitalism great. On the richest subcontinent in the world, with the largest production in agriculture, abundantly supplied with almost all raw materials, with an intelligent, educated, thrifty population, inheriting the unconquerable spirit of the frontier, united under one law and language and market, and with almost every circumstance in her favor, no wonder the United States rose to a unique position. No country in all history ever had such an opportunity. Two world wars that left the rest of the world impoverished only enriched the United States. We entered World War I as the world's biggest debtor nation and emerged from that war as the world's leading creditor country. Though strangely backward in many respects in culture, in character, and in spiritual qualities, America is today the richest nation on earth, capable of the largest production the world has ever known, and with the responsibility of assuming world leadership to help other nations gain or regain their footing.

As I have shuttled back and forth for sixty years among thirty nations, I have been able to see my own beloved country more objectively and impartially than if I had never left it. From a world viewpoint I find that Americans are practical, utilitarian, efficient, mechanical, often materialistic, progressive, adaptable, courageous, adventuresome, generous, philanthropic, moral, and religious. These qualities are almost ideal characteristics for world leadership.

But I find also that, compared to Europeans, Americans are adolescent, immature, isolationist in tendency, hypersensitive to criticism, often crude, sometimes vulgar, lacking in culture, sentimental, emotional, in certain situations hysterical, mob-minded in crises, with a bad record in graft and crime from the time of George Washington to Senator Kefauver. I find all these traits confirmed by Professor Henry Steele Commager after he has lived, lectured, and journeyed much abroad, and by other liberals.

There have been great economic and social tensions in our country, and my eyes were opened to one of them—the plight of the sharecroppers in the South—through an experience with violence in Arkansas. With my fellow worker, Sam Franklin, of Tennessee, I visited Arkansas and Mississippi in the spring of 1936 to investigate the predicament of evicted tenant farmers. The first day we saw aspects of slavery, feudalism, and Fascism in the attitude of the planters and landowners toward the evicted sharecroppers and tenant farmers, both black and white. The ordinary sharecropper in Arkansas was then receiving an average income of $212 a year per family. Twenty-five thousand of these poorest sharecroppers had formed the Tenant Farmers' Union, which was bitterly opposed by the landowners and planters, who were genuinely alarmed lest it liberate these men from the existing system of peonage and semi-slavery. The result was that scores of families, white and black, had been evicted from their farms and homes, this wholesale eviction being the weapon used to check the growth of the Union. I went out from Memphis with several friends, including a professor of the University, to visit one colored colony of recently evicted families. Within half an hour after we had arrived at the tent colony and had begun to investigate conditions we were arrested by Deputy Sheriffs Tip Sullivan and J. W. Shelby of Parkin, Cross County, Arkansas. We were taken to a large cotton store and locked in for two hours, while a score of planters and leading men were brought in to tell us "the truth about these damned niggers who won't work." They bitterly resented our coming from other states, seemingly to interfere with their victims and their own "state's rights."

Further investigation revealed appalling conditions among tenant farmers in several other states. Standards of living were disgracefully low, undernourishment was widely prevalent, and virtual peonage was practiced across wide areas. We decided that something should be done at once; at least a beginning might be made to challenge this system of peonage and help these farmers to achieve a better standard of living, a liberated life. We bought a farm on the spot, raised $17,500 in thirty days and paid cash for the 2138 acres which we called Rochdale, located south of Memphis in the Mississippi Delta, near Hillhouse, in Bolivar County, Mississippi. Within a few months thirty evicted families were settled on the farm. Then Cooperative Farms, Inc., was formed with Reinhold Niebuhr as president, myself as secretary-treasurer, Sam H. Franklin, Jr., as director, and Bishop William Scarlett, John Rust, and William Amberson as trustees. Response to the public appeal for financial assistance was so generous that within a year the farm was clear of indebtedness, and improvements to the extent of $30,000 had been made.

In 1939 a second farm, the Providence Cooperative Farm, was purchased on the edge of the Delta in Holmes County. Activities were gradually transferred to Providene, and the Delta Rochdale Farm was sold in 1942 for $34,000 cash. The history of the project for the next decade was one of constant struggle in the midst of bitter race prejudice, a mixture of failure and success, and of sacrificial service rendered by volunteer workers from near and far. The war, which brought relative prosperity to cotton workers as it did to farmers generally, disrupted many activities and resulted in the loss of farm families and staff members. After a checkered history, this collective, or producers' co-operative, had been dropped, and the land is being operated by individual families. But for fifteen years some of us had thrilling adventures in fighting lawlessness, race prejudice, and poverty in one of the most backward states in the deep South. We pioneered in a number of experiments that were later copied in more elaborate government projects undertaken by the New Deal. The publicity regarding our farm and the Southern Tenant Farmers' Union during this period of violence and dire poverty helped to focus the attention of the country on the South, which, in the words of President Roosevelt, was "the nation's number one economic problem." Conditions have been slowly but radically improved throughout Mississippi, both economically and in race relations. Our experience seems to confirm that of others in the past that a consumers' co-operative store, or a credit co-operative, if conducted on sound lines on the Rochdale plan, is usually successful. But it also seemed to show that producers' co-operatives, whether in agriculture or in industry, have practically always failed in the free world, as a century ago Emerson and Hawthorne found at Brook Farm and Fruitlands and Robert Owen at New Harmony, Indiana. One of the important continuing features of our Providence Cooperative Farm is the Medical Clinic, under the able direction of Dr. David R. Minter. Having treated over twelve thousand patients, mostly Negroes, Dr. Minter is still treating them at the rate of some fifty a day in his new clinic. The work of A. E. Cox as director has also been efficient and devoted.

I have become increasingly aware of the disastrous practice of lumping together in a single category varied types of social change. For thirty years I have been trying to help people recognize the differences between old-line predatory capitalism, New Dealism, Fair Dealism, Norman Thomas socialism, Earl Browder-Eugene Dennis Communism, and American neo-Fascism. Constantly I have combated the widespread habit of labeling all departures from orthodox capitalism as "red" or communistic. From the days of the Lusk Committee of the New York State Legislature to the House Committe on Un-American Activities and Senator McCarthy, the practice has prevailed of looking upon socialists and liberals and pacifists as "subversive," "red," and "communistic."

I have myself often been the victim of this practice. Countless times the charge has been made that I am a Communist, or at least a fellow traveler. This falsifying has not been stopped by constant affirmation and reiteration in my addresses, pamphlets, articles, and books that it is morally impossible for me as a Christian to be a Communist or fellow traveler. I am proud that my name was included in *The Red Network*, edited by Elizabeth Dilling in 1934. Since this volume has been "the Bible" of organizations and individuals following the practice of lumping together socialists and liberals and pacifists, and because it is still being used as an authoritative source, let me point out certain things about it.

Among the organizations listed as "subversive" were the invaluable and courageous American Civil Liberties Union, the American Friends Service Committee (Quakers), the Catholic Association for International Peace, the Federal Council of the Churches of Christ in America, The Fellowship of Reconciliation, the Foreign Policy Association, National Catholic Welfare Conference, Union Theological Seminary, the YMCA and YWCA. Among individuals listed as "reds" were Jane Addams, Secretary of War Newton D. Baker, Senator William E. Borah, S. Parkes Cadman, S. M. Cavert, John Dewey,

Paul H. Douglas (now Senator), Albert Einstein, Harry Emerson Fosdick, Felix Frankfurter (now Justice), Mahatma Gandhi, Charles W. Gilkey, Lynn Harold Hough, Paul Hutchinson, Senator La Follette, Rabbi Louis L. Mann, Bishop F. J. McConnell, Charles Clayton Morrison, Reinhold Niebuhr, Mrs. Franklin D. Roosevelt, Bishop William Scarlett, Luther A. Weigle, and Rabbi Stephen S. Wise. Though unworthy, I am proud to belong to such an honor roll.

This smearing of liberals and pacifists has reached its culmination in the actions of Senator McCarthy. With skill and ruthlessness he has used the device of guilt by association, guilt by accusation, by character assassination, by insinuation and falsification. He early discovered the technique of the "big lie" in his smear campaigns. In the *Congressional Record* for February 20, 1950, he said in almost succeeding sentences, "vast numbers of other Communists" (in the State Department), "over 200," "the names of 57 Communists," "the cases number 81," and then: "I know absolutely of one group of approximately 300 certified to the Secretary [to be] discharged because of Communism." Up to the moment of writing *he has failed to prove the guilt of a single case*—whether 205, 57, 81, 200, 300, or finally even "one chief Russian spy." Further, he has attacked in turn three of the most distinguished men in America, switching from Professor Owen Lattimore of Johns Hopkins University, to Dr. Philip C. Jessup, and then to a sixty-thousand-word violent, bitter, and false attack on General George C. Marshall, former Secretary of State, Chief of Staff and Nobel Prize winner, as a traitor who "had always supported

Soviet interest." I could literally fill a whole chapter with an account of innocent people who have suffered, lost their positions or their reputations by the lies and gratuitous, unproved accusations of Senator McCarthy and his hench-men. I was proud of the defense made by my former pri-vate secretary, Bishop G. Bromley Oxnam, in his *I Protest,* after his eventful twelve-hour day before the committee. He truly says: "This is not an investigation. It is intimida-tion. It is a 20th-century inquisition."

I hope McCarthy will soon pass from the scene as did Huey Long—whom I knew personally and who was our one potential Hitler in his day. I mention McCarthy only as a symptom of moral degradation in America. I believe, however, that as Germany reached an all-time low in Hitler, and Russia in Stalin, McCarthy marks an all-time moral low in our own country.

Readers of Alan Bullock's *Hitler: A Study in Tyranny* must have been struck, as was President Eisenhower's brother, by the many similarities between Hitler and McCarthy. Both were nominal Roman Catholics, though neither gave evidence of believing in God or man. Neither had the advantage of a wholesome, happy home life. Both were attacking Communism and each professed to be the savior of his country from this dire evil. Both used the method of violent vituperation, and both seized the initiative by repeated attacks against every opponent, often without offering evidence and without bothering to defend their own falsehoods. Both had ability, both were clever charlatans, both were able speakers, both despised the lack of intelligence of the common people and believed they could command a following and increase the national hysteria that would bring them into such power that they would never have to justify the false and evil means they had used. The same ugly rumors persisted concerning the top associates of both Hitler and McCarthy. Both had a consuming ambition for power and believed that the end justified any means whatever.

Upon his return to the United States, Dr. Roswell P. Bates, speaker of the Maine House of Representatives, a member of our Seminar in Europe in 1953, stated in the Bangor *Commercial* that out of sixty-six speakers heard by the Seminar in all of Europe, fifty raised the issue of McCarthyism in criticism of America. Adlai Stevenson in his journey around the world had the same experience. Both men found that McCarthy had lowered American prestige all over the world, as the representatives of our State Department in all countries have reported.

Perhaps the most serious aspect of the present crisis in our national affairs is the fact that a man of this character and with this record could be elected to high office by the vote of the people. The man himself is a revelation of the gullibility, the passions, the fears, the hysteria, the moral callousness of many citizens. In attacking McCarthy we are really indicting ourselves. I have been amazed at the number of reputable Republicans since Senator Taft, some of them earnest professing Christians, who have been blind to the inevitable moral results of using the slanders of Senator McCarthy for the advantage of cheap party politics.

We must be on guard, however, against bitterness and contempt for our fellow men. I am convinced by overwhelming evidence, confirmed by fearless articles by Justice Douglas and our best commentators, that Senator McCarthy is a national menace. I do not hate but I have pitied and abhorred Hitler, Stalin, and McCarthy and shall fight against their influence to my last breath.

In striving to build a new America I agree with the transparently devout Roman Catholic, Father James Keller, in his recent book, *You Can Change the World.* Father Keller shows that less that one per cent of our population are gangsters, criminals and Communists, intent on tearing down our social order. He pleads for another one per cent as "Christophers," of Christ-bearers, to overcome these forces of evil and play a part in building the new America and the new world. If real Christians, Catholic and Protestant, and all liberals and decent people can thus unite we can indeed build a new America.

Chapter 9

❦

LIVING IN A REVOLUTIONARY WORLD

As I look back over sixty years of travel in thirty lands, the outstanding characteristic of the whole period seems to me to be *revolution*. I have watched two men lead two great revolutions in the twentieth century—Lenin and Gandhi. The one, with clenched fist, mounting a gun carriage in Petrograd where his monument now stands, called for a revolution of blood and iron on the part of the workers of the world and forged a totalitarian government under which millions have perished and other millions are still enslaved. The other, sitting cross-legged upon the floor, turning his spinning wheel—symbol of freedom for one-fifth of the human race—conducted a revolution of nonviolence based upon the principle of love.

From the time the British East India Company entered India in 1600 some of the English, at their best, had always visioned a future when India would realize its freedom. The British with their *Pax Britannica* found it possible to prepare India for self-government and independence, although the process was neither uniform nor continuous. The great Macaulay, when he made English rather than Sanskrit the basis of India's educational system, foresaw this possible demand for liberty as "the proudest day in England's history."

When I landed in India in 1896 the revolution had already begun in both its industrial and its political aspects. Under the watchword *Swadeshi*, meaning "own country," a boycott movement was under way in which Indians refused to buy British manufactures in order to develop their own homemade products—just as the American colonists had done. They initiated their own free industry by developing cotton fabrics and later founded Indian banks, steamship companies, iron and steel industries, air lines, and other commercial and industrial enterprises.

To match the commercial *Swadeshi* they rallied under the political watchword *Swaraj*, or self-government, seeking for forty years to achieve Dominion status like Canada—to become a self-governing member of the British Empire. Both the industrial and the political revolutions were to be realized through the National Congress, an unofficial, self-appointed Duma where political leaders met to discuss in English their national problems and present their grievances to their British rulers.

I came to admire British rule in India and I know of no finer instance in history of the government of one people by another. But the British failed to realize the warning of Sir John Seely in *The Expansion of England*: "Subjection for a long time to a foreign yoke is one of the most potent causes of national deterioration." Through self-interest the British, like all imperialists, were blind to this truth; but Gandhi realized it in his very soul and took it as his text.

In spite of admiration for the British I came to have a growing sympathy for the Indian Nationalist drive for self-government. The protests and the reforms of the Nationalists were logical. Take their spinning-wheel campaign. The cotton plant was native to India, and until the eighteenth century India had supplied Europe with its finest cotton goods. Then Britain allowed Lancaster to kill India's profitable cottage industry by imposing a 75 per cent tax on Indian cotton goods imported into Britain. After the development of English factories, it was cheaper for the Indians themselves to buy goods manufactured in England. Gandhi introduced the spinning wheel to teach the people to make their own homespun clothing again, to save millions of dollars in foreign trade, and to build backbone for a self-governing people in an effort to correct the moral "national deterioration." In the same way each of Gandhi's reforms was grounded in a passionate moral issue, with far greater justification than the American colonies' relatively trifling protest against the Stamp Act or the tax on tea.

I had many close and personal contacts with the Indian leaders. At the close of 1929 I spent a memorable hour with the poet Tagore in his home. I was entertained in the palatial residence of Pandit Jawaharlal Nehru and then spent ten days with Gandhi at his ashram at Sabarmati. Also I attended the Lahore meeting of the National Congress. After interviewing some fifty Indian leaders I found none willing to continue under the existing relationship to Great Britain. Evidence to this fact was the 30,000 Indian political prisoners, whose number finally rose to 100,000. With Kirby Page I lunched with the Viceroy,

Lord Irwin (the present Lord Halifax). When he heard that we were on our way to visit Gandhi he asked us if we would take a message to him and obtain a reply. The English and the Indians were then rapidly drifting apart and both feared violence, so that the Viceroy was eager to come to an understanding with the Indian leaders.

Gandhi, sitting on the floor of his ashram, listened to the Viceroy's message and then gave his reply. In substance he said:

To be told that India is an equal, but on the level of a beloved child who has not yet reached the age of responsibility and of political majority, is not enough. We are offered Dominion status "in the fullness of time," but this leaves our fate solely to Britain's selfish imperialistic decision. Our position is clear. Unless our demand for Dominion status is accepted on or before December 31, 1929—that is, before the close of the coming Lahore meeting of the National Congress—we will be compelled, after vainly pleading for Dominion status for forty years, to declare for complete independence and organize a campaign of non-violent non-cooperation to obtain our freedom.

Early the next month, January, 1930, in the Lahore meeting I heard Gandhi move his resolution for complete independence before fifteen thousand delegates. His was no spread-eagle oratory—"Give me liberty or give me death." Rather he spoke like the gentle St. Francis of Assisi. But the vast audience seemed to hang upon his every word although he was so feeble from a weakened heart that he had to remain seated while he spoke. His ultimatums carried authority. The personal discipline of his own life and his devotion to the common good spoke to and for the people. I once heard the poetess, Her Excellency Sarojini

Naidu, Governor of the United Provinces, when unveiling a bust of Gandhi, give her estimate of the three greatest spiritual leaders of the human race: Jesus Christ, Gautama Buddha, Mahatma Gandhi. Millions in India agree with her.

Finally, in 1948 I saw the British Labor government fulfill Lord Macaulay's dream of "the proudest day in England's history" when it sent out Lord Mountbatten to liquidate the rule of the British Empire and permit the formation of the Republic of India. The following year, as a guest of the first Indian Governor-General, Rajagopalachariar, in his huge palace built by the British at Delhi, I went over to take lunch with the first Indian Prime Minister, my old friend Nehru. Within sixty years I had witnessed the complete sweep of the revolution in India.

On my last trip around the world in 1948–49 I made a final visit to the Orient, including twenty-six localities in India. On the whole I was gratified at the progress of India as a new republic. I was glad to see that many landlords led by Gandhi's disciple, Vinoba Bhave, had voluntarily contributed something like a million acres of land for distribution among the landless poor. I should have been much more gratified if the landowners in the Indian Parliament had been unselfish enough—and farsighted enough—to sell a portion of their holdings to the millions of landless peasants. The concentration of land in the hands of the wealthy has long been one of India's major injustices. At one time I witnessed in one district in Hyderabad a frightful land tyranny under the old grafter, the Nizam, who was said to be the richest man in the world. No wonder that during the three-year period prior to 1949 the Communists of this same district had gained adherents among the landless peasants by killing some three thousand landlords and their supporters in guerrilla warfare. I saw similar reprisals in parts of Pakistan, especially on the boundary of Afghanistan, where graft was far worse than in India.

It seems to me that the future of Asia hinges on India's response to Communism. From all I have seen, India seems relatively safe from actually going Communist, partly through her deep religious inheritance and also through absorption in building an independent republic. Nehru still seems to me the ablest statesman in Asia. India's safety lies in the fact that Nehru does not favor the rich landlords or take sides with capitalist America. He is intent upon meeting the needs of the common people. As Justice Douglas points out, nothing less than a welfare state, demanding justice for all, concerned with the impoverished masses and with "the people's livelihood" can possibly save India or any other land in Asia.

In 1949 as I attended the meetings of the Constituent Assembly, a Parliament in action, I was deeply impressed. The members seemed to be more highly educated and to act with more political sagacity than the legislators of any other Parliament I have seen in Asia. A large proportion were members of the Congress party, which emphasizes socialized industry; they wore white Gandhi caps and coarse cotton homespun. I was also impressed by the caliber of the cabinet of the central government. Two of the members were Christians, two were Moslems, one was a Sikh, two were from the former untouchables, one was a distinguished Indian woman.

Events move swiftly these days; anyone who prognosticates climbs out on a limb. Nevertheless I have traveled the seven seas long enough to know that the swells are more important to a ship's reckoning than the choppy surface waves. I dare to say that the swell in India evidences the ultimate realization of democracy.

Simultaneous with the revolution in India, one of a different nature was taking place in China. Over a period of more than forty years my work took me over the whole of that great country. I traveled in every sort of way: bullock cart, camel back, donkey, sedan chair, ricksha, automobile, truck, train and airplane, junk, sailboat, launch, and river steamer. No other land gives such an impression of its age-old past. When I saw the skull of "Peking man," half a million years old, and stood on the ancient drum towers of Peking looking down in imagination on the twenty-four long dynasties of the last four thousand years, I felt the pulsing of the past in the arteries of the new day. No other land gives such an impression of the simultaneousness of the centuries; one big reason why modern governments find such difficulty in functioning is that they must function for nomads as well as for twentieth-century technocrats.

Civilization is a hard word to define but as a state of social development an easy thing to sense, and as one becomes accustomed to Chinese life one feels that here is an innately civilized people. And yet some of the criteria by which Westerners characterize civilization are almost totally lacking. For instance, the Chinese have a defective sense of personal responsibility for public wrong. For a thousand years official graft has gone practically unchallenged, and one reason for its vitality has been the conservatism of the people—perhaps the most conservative people on earth. No wonder a revolution in China moves in slow convulsions.

When I first visited China in 1907 the corrupt and degenerate Manchus were still on the throne, last of the twenty-four dynasties. But by then the revolution was well under way. Potentially, as was said by a follower of Sun Yat-sen in 1911, China's revolution began in 1807 on the day Robert Morrison, the first Protestant missionary, stepped ashore in Canton. All unconsciously Morrison came with three bombs in his pocket—the disruptive force of a new religion, an explosive nationalism, and an industrial revolution. The second phase of the revolution was destructive, expressed through the Taiping rebellion, 1851–1864, which swept away some twenty millions in bloody slaughter in an attempt to stabilize the old ways and the old days, and later, in 1900, in the Boxer uprising, which tried also by slaughter to force all foreigners and their influence out of China. The destructive phase is now being completed in the purges, trials, and brain washings of the Communists.

In 1911 the revolution became articulate when Dr. Sun Yat-sen, after ten vain attempts, set up the republic and declared its ideals in the Three Principles of the People: nationalism, democracy, and livelihood. Temporarily the revolution and the republic met a setback in the counterrevolution of Yuan Shih-kai, who used his position as first President of the republic as a springboard for achieving his ambition to become Emperor. I have two Chinese dollars minted at the same time in 1915, one proclaiming

Yuan President of the republic and the other proclaiming him Emperor of a new dynasty. Fortunately he died before he could realize his greatest ambition.

It was fascinating to meet the successive leaders of China. I found Sun Yat-sen a patriotic revolutionary, deservedly called "the father of his country." Utterly impractical, he dreamed of a republic he could never build. And yet he had tremendous tenacity; he did found the republic! I felt that Yuan Shih-kai was a more powerful and attractive personality but an ignorant pagan war lord who had no conception of the real revolution, or of a republic, or a democracy.

I knew Marshal Feng, "the Christian general," well all during the days of his ascendancy when he, like Chiang Kai-shek, was widely heralded by the missionaries because he was a Christian. He had become a Christian in Peking in 1912 when he attended a meeting conducted by John R. Mott. Feng was a winsome, lovable man, in spite of the fact that he had been schooled by the old regime to hate all foreigners. He told me that at the turn of the century he had been stationed by the Governor of Shantung at Patotingfu, the city in which my roommate Pitkin had been beheaded, ostensibly to protect the missionaries but in reality to make sure that not a single "foreign devil" escaped. When I knew Feng some ten thousand of his troops had become Christians. Like Cromwell's Ironsides his men might neither drink, smoke, nor gamble but went marching through the streets singing "Onward Christian Soldiers." Daily at 7:30 A.M. after their drill I met nearly a thousand of his Christian officers, each with his pocket notebook and New Testament, for a Bible class. Like

Gandhi, Feng himself rose at four and after his devotions studied Chinese and English. Several times he turned to Moscow as his last hope of obtaining help, but he finally repudiated Communist cruelties and in indignation told Borodin, his Russian adviser, to leave China. Feng was like a village Cromwell, but without education; he had a peasant mind that often plunged on impulse, alternating between his Oriental and Occidental loyalties to persons or principles, unable consistently to save China.

When Chiang Kai-shek became the new "Christian general" of China, he felt himself to be China's man of destiny. He had the least attractive personality of any national leader I ever met, though Stilwell was unjustified in calling him contemptuously "the peanut." I found him to be silent, masterful, strong-willed, and stubborn. He was characterized by tenacity, decision, energy, ambition, political shrewdness, an inveterate habit of compromise, and a deep love of power. He usually won his battles against a score of ruthless war lords with "silver bullets," or bribery, and fought with lead bullets only when he had to.

Nevertheless Chiang Kai-shek was Dr. Sun's spiritual son, and in his early days he made an all-out attempt to unite China. There was a time in the late twenties when he appeared to have succeeded, but to effect the union he had had to admit Communist advisers and cabinet members into his inner circle. Be it said to his credit, he was the first first-water national leader to realize that no government can do business with Communism and remain an independent government. This point of view he doggedly adhered to even during his war with Japan, consistently attempting to tell his foreign advisers that the last state of

China would be worse than the first if he placed armed power in Communist hands, that a Communist-dominated China would have even less fruit than a Japanese-dominated China. For practical purposes, Chiang never united China. The forces against him were too vast, the force within him too weak.

I met him in 1931 and again in 1934. In 1931 I had just addressed the Governor of Hupeh at Wuchang with two hundred of his officials and officers. I showed them a map of their province with six-sevenths of the area marked in red, territory then in the hands of either Communists or bandits. I charged them with having caused this condition by robbing not only the rich by their graft but also the half-starving flood refugees whom they were responsible for feeding. The Governor admitted all my charges regarding graft. Later when I laid the case before Chiang he demoted the Governor only one grade—to be commanding general of the troops—and the graft went on as before, with Chiang's knowledge.

Again in 1934 I called Chiang's attention to the corrupt Governor Liu Hsiang of Szechuan. To enrich himself this Governor had been selling opium to his entire province and to his rotten army, many of whom had become opium sots. In some counties Liu had collected the land tax thirty, forty, and even sixty years before it was due. I took an airplane and got to the Generalissimo at his military capital of Nanchang a day before Governor Liu arrived. I showed Chiang on a map of Szechwan where the 80,000 Communist troops were then said to be located in the north of the province, and the disposition of the 300,000 Nationalist soldiers according to the briefing I had received from the

Szechuan generals. I told the Generalissimo that there would have to be immediate and drastic measures of reform or the Communists would set up in the West their "Soviet Republic of China." Once again Chiang compromised, made Liu Hsiang the commander of the troops of Szechuan, and the system of bribery and corruption continued as before.

Finally, in 1948 I flew to Formosa and witnessed the disgraceful misrule there, immediately following the encumbency of Governor Chen Yi, who had been appointed by Chiang. The Governor had answered the Formosans' demands for some measure of justice and liberty by a massacre of five thousand of their people, including every leading Formosan whom he could seize. I admit that Chiang now has a new and better army in Formosa, a new and better government, but three times I have seen him organize a new army and a new government and three times I have seen him fail. The cause of failure is in himself.

It takes no prophet to foresee what will happen if Chiang's forces invade the mainland of China. They may make a few hit-and-run guerrilla raids but they will be defeated in real battles as they always were. If they have sufficient nuisance value they may force the Communists to bomb Formosa. I am confident, however, that our President will not involve us in an atomic World War III with either China or Russia, a war that no one could win, which would leave the cities of both the USA and the USSR devastated.

I have always been concerned not only with the political and military struggle in China but even more with the divided religious allegiance of the Chinese people. Despite the early values of Buddhism, Confucianism, and Taoism, it seems to me that all have tended to arrest China's development. In our day it seems obvious that none of these ancient religions had the dynamic to build a new China.

But within the past century two foreign religions have appeared, each of which believed it could build a new China: Christianity and Communism. Christianity claimed to have converted the crumbling Roman Empire and laid the moral foundations for Western civilization in Europe and America. Christians believed they could rebuild China in the same way by a voluntary, evolutionary, educational process. The Communists believed that Christianity had failed to administer justice through the system that they called "capitalistic imperialism," and that this system would either fall because of its internal contradictions or be overthrown by force as it had been in Czarist Russia.

Just as I have tried fairly to discern things both good and bad in Russia as I saw them under Lenin and Stalin, so I have tried to find the good and the bad behind the bamboo curtain in Communist China today. My friends who have lived under Communist rule in China report that whereas the Kuomintang in its brutality merely killed men's bodies, the Communists, despite their economic reforms, often kill the spirit of men if they deem them enemies. They say the Communist regime inherits many evils derived from Marx, such as its atheism and its harsh dictatorship. In addition it has taken on many of the characteristics of the Russian police state, such as its mass trials, its forced morbid confessions, its ruthless purges and consequent widespread fear and suspicion. The cruel and degrading process of "brain washing" has often been conducted by ignorant men and propagandists upon both foreigners and Chinese. No individual has any rights before the absolute Communist state. The intellectual worker or teacher must continually reveal his mind to the authorities under a rigid "thought control." The system seems to be destroying many of the human values built up through long centuries of both Confucianism and Christianity.

All of these things being true, many Americans, as well as the American press, seem to feel it is disloyal to admit any good trait in Communist China. However, my friends in China inform me that while all the evils I have mentioned do characterize the Communist regime, it has nevertheless launched a score of desperately needed reforms. A land reform, however ruthless, has at last materialized, and half the country's land has been divided among some forty million of the landless peasants, who consequently defend the regime that gave them the land. Inflation, long the bane of China, has at last been controlled. For the first time the "people's livelihood" has been taken seriously and the government seems determined to realize a higher standard of living for all. The age-long curse of graft and corruption has been largely swept away. Taxes, though high, now go into the government coffers. Banditry, which has been widespread since the war-lord period, has markedly decreased. Laws made in the capital, Peiping, are now administered in the remotest village.

Many of these facts were confirmed by the report of the United Nations Economic Commission for Asia and the Far East in 1953. Half the cultivated land of China

has been distributed to 90 per cent of the peasants in small
holdings. Nationalization has extended to 80 per cent of
heavy industry and 90 per cent of light industry. The government operates all railways and 60 per cent of the steam-
ships ; is responsible for half of the wholesale and 30 per
cent of the retail trade ; controls 90 per cent of all loans
and deposits. And 90 per cent of the rural population
appear to have benefited by the agrarian reforms.

There is a new enthusiasm for a new way of life, especially among the youth. The Chinese have recovered confidence in themselves and "millions feel that they are living for the first time." The incoming Communist regime
was indignant at the inferior position of women under the
system of Confucius. Jack Belden, in his book *China Shakes
the World,* shows that the Chinese Communists did more
in two years to stop wife-beating than did all other forces
combined since the time of Confucius. In their effort to
change the character of the Chinese people the Communists are ruthlessly exterminating "face," fate, favor, nepo-
tism—the old evils described by Lin Yutang as having so
long corrupted Chinese life—together with the gentle
streak of feminism in Chinese character. Dr. Sun Yat-sen
almost despaired of his people because, while the Japanese
were a monolithic unity, he said the Chinese were a "loose
heap of sand." But just as in the heart of the earth under
terrific heat and pressure sand becomes rock, so the Chinese are being solidified by the heat and pressure of the
forces working on them.

We cannot yet verify all the reports coming from China,
either good or bad. It is too early to give a final evaluation
to Communist domination. But the twenty-sixth dynasty,

Communism, claims the right of evolution by revolution that was justified by Mencius twenty-two centuries ago. It must make good or perish as the preceding twenty-five dynasties have. I believe God's purpose for China has not yet been achieved, but I believe it will be achieved in time. As Christians we are going to have to continue to do what we have done before in our wiser moments—accept the good in our enemy, love him in spite of horrendous faults, pray God to cleanse, purify, and bless him, develop in ourselves humility, faith, and the will to manifest the brotherhood to which we subscribe.

In Japan I have found that the nation's development has been more evolutionary than revolutionary. Like the British, the Japanese are a law-abiding people. Loyal to their sovereign and their national leaders, they are the most patriotic and united people in the world. Japan was the first Oriental nation to industrialize and absorb Western civilization. She was the one nation I have observed in Asia which was quick to learn, rapidly able to compete with the West on its own ground at almost every point. With an area and resources less than the single state of California, lacking in almost all essential raw materials, and having little more than a tenth of the wealth and income of the United States, Japan attempted the impossible and lifted herself by her own bootstraps.

In two Japanese men I saw typified and embodied Japan's mighty achievements in a single generation. The first was Viscount Shibusawa, the aged financier and grand old man of Japan who by the age of ninety had witnessed the transformation of his people during his own lifetime. He told me that he was a boy of thirteen when

Commodore Perry's fleet of American gunboats first arrived in 1853, then returned the following year after Japan had opened her long-closed doors to modern trade. At that time Shibusawa believed that the world was a solid cube and on its flat top were only four countries: Japan, Korea, China, and India. After Perry's arrival he had to enlarge his flat world and to add two more lands, America and a country called Europe.

At that time he told me he was in favor of resisting the American fleet, but when the shot fired from the rusty Japanese battery on the shore splashed harmlessly in the water about halfway to its destination, he changed his mind. Japan offered no other resistance to the gradual opening of the door to the Western World. Shibusawa saw Japan transformed by the whole complex of Western civilization. He witnessed a political revolution, an intellectual renaissance, and an industrial and social reorganization of his country almost unparalleled in history. He became Japan's leading banker, held office as president, director, or adviser of some sixty corporations, and was identified with scores of philanthropic and social welfare organizations.

The second man I observed was Prince Tokugawa, president of the House of Peers, a lineal descendant of the great shoguns who had ruled Japan for two and a half centuries and banished Christianity in bloodshed from the land. In 1868 he was a boy of five, when the shogunate fell and all the 262 feudal lords surrendered their fiefs, and the boy Emperor took the great Charter Oath. He witnessed the amazing progress of Japan in industrial and military power during the forty-five years of the new Meiji era. In 1922 he was his country's representative at the Washington Disarmament Conference, which sought to avert World War II by restricting the fleets of the Western powers and of Japan on a ratio of 5 : 5 : 3. Prince Tokugawa's constant effort for closer international friendship and his repeated testimony as to the value of Christianity to Japan were a striking evidence of how far his country had traveled during his short lifetime—from complete isolation, reactionary feudalism, and the absolute prohibition of Christianity as a dangerous foreign religion to openminded co-operation on all fronts.

In 1948 when I landed in the new revolutionary Asia, I seemed to be witnessing the birth of a new Japan—a new democracy, a new constitution, and at first sight almost a new people. Naturally I contrasted all this with the old semifeudal Japan that I had known forty years earlier.

For the first time in history our country had embarked on the unique experiment of seeking to rebuild a conquered nation, not according to its own past, but following the bold blueprints of modern democracy. One of the first projected reforms was the new Japanese land act. The land reform law aimed to make nine-tenths of the peasants landowners, an important change in a country with the greatest population pressure of any in the world, excepting Java. Within a month of the surrender of Japan the Supreme Commander, General MacArthur, announced as a second reform that he would "favor a program for the dissolution of the large industrial and banking combines." Formerly the Zaibatsu, or money clique, included the four great combines—Mitsui, Mitsubishi,

Sumitomo, and Yasuda—and controlled the bulk of the industry, transportation, banking, and economic activity of old Japan.

By 1948 the labor movement, constantly suppressed by Imperial Japan, had been reorganized and was making giant strides with the help of labor advisers from America. The old Home Ministry had been dissolved with its loathed secret police, who sought to control not only all "dangerous thought" but the entire life of the people. SCAP [1] optimistically claimed that the third year of the occupation marked the fulfillment of nearly all the major occupation objectives. The best of all the reforms were written into the new constitution.

The greatest Japanese I have known in all my visits to Japan was the Christian leader Toyohiko Kagawa. His views of the American occupation seemed to me typical of the most trustworthy opinion. He said to me:

Japan today is undergoing an unparalleled radical social and political revolution. Defeat has made us a new nation. When the Emperor acknowledged defeat on August 15, 1945, the mythology of Japan was shattered (concerning the sun goddess and the divine descent and destiny of the Emperor and the people of Japan, who were thereby destined for the conquest of Asia and the world). Japan's defeat in the war would have brought on a bloody revolution, as it did in Germany and in Russia, were it not for the American Occupation's giving food to the Japanese people and striving not to crush but to reform their feudal condition. Japan welcomed the American army of liberation which set my country free from the fatal program of the militarists.

MacArthur has been amazing; future Japan will owe much to him. But the total revolution taking place is the resultant of three

[1] Supreme Command of the Army of the Pacific.

forces—war, the American Occupation, and the Japanese character. I gladly welcome the revolution's ten principal achievements: 1. The denial by the Emperor of divinity and the firm establishment of the principle that sovereignty shall reside in the people. This is embodied in the new Constitution which begins: "We the people . . . do ordain and establish." 2. The legal recognition of labor unions. 3. The abolition of the centuries-old prostitution system. 4. The renunciation of the right of belligerency. 5. The emancipation of the peasant class by the establishment of the Farm Land Readjustment Law. 6. The firm establishment of freedom of thought. 7. The emancipation of women and granting them the franchise. 8. The Livelihood Security Law. 9. The checks and balances of a legislative, executive and judicial system of government. 10. The emergence of a Liberal-Social Democratic cabinet. I must add, of course, the effort to undergird these reforms by a democratic system of education.

Had it not been for the defeat of Japan, the above reforms would not have been realized in less than one or two centuries. The golden age of capitalism has gone. Defeat has compelled us to begin to socialize our economy. But although we are in the midst of an economic and political revolution, we have yet to see a spiritual revolution in needy Japan.

The highest privilege I enjoyed in Japan was the hour my wife and I spent with the Emperor and Empress. I felt that we were talking to a prisoner of his own past, only recently taken from behind the bars of an age-old formalism. We felt also that there was greater hope in the young Crown Prince, then being so wisely educated by the well-chosen American Quaker, Mrs. Elizabeth Gray Vining. The Emperor was greatly touched by our statement that he was more deeply intrenched in the loyal affection of his people than at any other time in his life. I told him that when Mrs. Uemura, a distinguished Christian Japanese lady, had recently been in the United States she had kept an impassive face in talking of the bombing of Tokyo and some seventy cities in a holocaust of fire, but that when she described the sufferings of the Emperor she had wept. On hearing this the Emperor bowed his head in silence.

All the problems of Japan have by no means been solved. It is evident, however, that there has been a very real gain in liberty and an advance in economic justice for the Japanese people. I hope that Japan is slowly but steadily moving toward a complete democracy that will be realized by evolution without violence among this law-abiding people.

Upon arrival in eastern Asia in 1948 we seemed to be witnessing the birth of a new Korea. Fifty years ago the heads both of patriots and of criminals impaled upon stakes by the roadside were evidence of a corrupt, irresponsible, and autocratic government. The last degenerate King had filled the country's unspeakable prisons and torture chambers with young reformers. The King robbed the nobles and the nobles robbed the peasants. The Korean people, in the opinion of their best friends, were at that time admitted to be "ignorant, corrupt, lazy, and superstitious." No man could say that of them today.

For half a century Korea had been the storm center of a triangle of the three giant powers of the Far East: China, Japan, and Russia. The United States, inexperienced in world leadership, never seemed to realize Korea's strategic importance. Watching Japan fight two wars to possess this Hermit Kingdom we should have recognized that it was at least full of potentialities if not of dynamite.

As all the world now knows, in 1944 at Yalta Korea

was arbitrarily though necessarily divided at the thirty-eighth parallel for the purpose of accepting the Japanese surrender, with the Russian army temporarily assigned to North and the American army to South Korea. The Russians then quickly set up a puppet government in the North. They early announced a Land Reform Law claiming to distribute 2,625,000 acres of land to 724,522 families, or 72 per cent of the farming families of North Korea. It was soon found, however, that no man held title to his land or could make disposition of his crops. The North quickly became a police state patterned after the usual Soviet tyranny.

The American occupation of Korea, which began on September 8, 1945, and ended officially on August 15, 1948, was regarded from the first as a short-term, caretaker job. Militarily, the forces left in the country as a training unit were vastly inadequate for defense, but actual defense was not envisaged. Politically, the Americans were slow in getting under way, especially when compared with the Communist manner of arriving on the scene with a full-blown governmental system. In the matter of social-economic services the Americans were much more adept. I was proud to observe that by generous grants the United States had prevented mass starvation. A system of free democratic education had been adopted, and trainees in many specialized and technical branches were sent to America for advanced training. There was marked improvement in public health and welfare. Principles of genuine democracy were embodied in the constitution of the new republic, in its Parliament, which I observed in action, and in the transfer to the Korean government of legislative, executive, and judicial functions. Ninety per cent of the qualified voters cast ballots in the first general election, and a new womanhood was emerging.

Then on Sunday, June 25, 1950, Russia's puppet state of North Korea, using Russian equipment and tanks, launched a long-prepared aggressive attack upon the Republic of South Korea. It was similar to Hitler's invasion of helpless Poland. Russian propaganda, blaring from Moscow, Berlin, and Peiping, was ready with its "big lie" that John Foster Dulles, currently visiting in Japan and Korea, had encouraged the South Koreans to attack the North, promising that the Americans would leap into the fray and fight their battles for them. Fortunately, the United Nations' Commission on Korea was already on the spot, had visited the border along the thirty-eighth parallel the very day before the attack, and could testify to the world that the southern republic was utterly unprepared, that it had made no attack, and that the invasion from the North had been an act of inexcusable, naked aggression.

I believe history will record that President Truman, meeting with the Secretaries of State and Defense and their staffs, took efficient and prompt action in placing General Douglas MacArthur in command and ordering all available American troops sent to Korea. The United Nations Security Council also met promptly and voted, nine to nothing, that "all members should render every assistance to the United Nations in repulsing this imperialistic act of aggression." Soon some twenty nations sent at least token forces to Korea, and the flags of fifty-three countries were represented there under the flag of the United Nations.

It is true that the United States had to furnish nine-tenths of the fighting forces and had an equal proportion of the casualties, but it was of immense moment that representatives of almost the whole free world were now defending an invaded nation. It was also a precedent of great promise that the nations could rally so promptly to defend one of their number when attacked, because the Soviet Union might try similar tactics in its future policy of world conquest.

In a strange way, however, in contrast to our brilliant record in Japan, Korea seemed to be for Americans a land of fatal mistakes. General John Reed Hodge, an honest soldier recently returned from his victories in Okinawa, began the American occupation of Korea with a series of stupid blunders. Then, after the Communist invasion of the southern republic, President Truman made his great mistake. In a conference with the press, in answer to a question whose import he did not quickly grasp he said casually that our government had considered the use of the atomic bomb in the Korean war, but that the final decision as to its use would be left to General Douglas MacArthur in the field. All Europe was stunned![2]

Then General MacArthur made his more serious mistakes, which further alarmed Europe. His gratuitous and flamboyant message to the Veterans of Foreign Wars en-

---

[2] When I saw Professor Harold Laski in London just before his death, he said to me: "If World War III comes as an atomic war, you may escape over the wide-open continental spaces of North America and Soviet Russia, but civilization would perish in Great Britain. We were almost bombed out of existence by Hitler's guided missiles in the last war, but in what would probably become a battle field our cities in the British Isles would be almost completely blotted out." It is against this background that European reaction to American policy must always be judged. General MacArthur was about the last man on earth to whom Europe was willing to trust its fate.

campment in Wisconsin was in opposition to the declared policy of his government, which was to keep the war in the Orient localized in Korea. That message enabled Chinese General Wu Hsiu-chuan to say to the nations at Lake Success that the United States had instigated the war in Korea to cover up "its fanatical design of dominating Asia and the world. . . . *The real intention of the United States, as MacArthur has confessed, is to dominate every Asiatic port from Vladivostok to Singapore.*"

The next mistake of MacArthur occurred when he disregarded the warning of the Chinese Premier and the fears of our European allies, crossed the thirty-eighth parallel, and drove on to the border of Manchuria. China immediately responded with her "million-man army," drove us back again to the south, and MacArthur admitted he had "an entirely new war" upon his hands. Walter Lippmann points out that MacArthur's failure to make an armistice and his attempt to occupy North Korea, thus dragging China with her unlimited man power into the conflict, was the fatal mistake of the whole Korean war.

Americans have been particularly blind in Asia. It is a continent of colored races justly resenting the white man's arrogance and his recent colonial rule. At one moment the world press announced that ex-President Hoover asked us to abandon to its fate both Europe and Asia, and in the next General MacArthur lightheartedly suggested launching vast bombing operations in Asia which might precipitate World War III.

When I interviewed General MacArthur I received the impression that he was an able commander and that his occupation measures in Japan were almost a work of genius. His faults, however, were equally transparent. He was obviously hypersensitive to criticism. Of all the world leaders I have met in the last sixty years I have never known one, not even Bernard Shaw, who was so manifestly suffering from megalomania, had such an inflated sense of his own greatness. Bernard Shaw might compare Shakespeare unfavorably with himself, but it was always with a broad smile and a keen sense of humor. But the megalomania of poor MacArthur was unrelieved by any sense of humor.

When peace is declared—not an armistice but genuine peace—Korea will be the most devastated country on earth and it will have to build new foundations amid ashes and rubble. There is evidence, however, that the revolution in Korea had made sufficient progress before it was halted by the invading army so that once peace is realized it can be hopefully resumed. Granted the necessary help from America and the United Nations, there is promise that in time Korea will be built into a republic firmly established upon foundations of economic justice and democratic liberty.

Almost the whole history of the revolution in Korea is embodied in one man, its first President, Syngman Rhee. Because he has been a personal friend for forty-two years I may be partial to him. To me he has always seemed to resemble his great teacher at Princeton, Woodrow Wilson. Both men believed profoundly in democratic principles, but both were autocratic and stubborn in temperament and in practice. I make no apology for Rhee's highhanded methods, for his too great reliance upon the police, or for

his insistence upon war, but I know no other man in
Korea prepared by experience or ability to take his
place.

Syngman Rhee was born on April 26, 1875. He studied
in an American Methodist institution, but as a "superior
man" of the Confucian tradition he proudly resisted the
religion of the foreigners. He began his career in politics
as a young journalist and started the first daily newspaper
in Korea, in which he opposed the reactionary regime of
the last effete Korean Emperor, Yi Hiung (or Rhee
Hiung), to whom he was personally related. When he and
a score of modern educated young liberals formed the New
Independence party and began advocating a constitutional
government, they were thrown into prison. They were held
in an ancient, verminous, and filthy dungeon, and all were
subject to torture. Rhee's friend, Kim, had his leg broken.
After each period of torture, Rhee himself was bound
hand and foot in the stocks. Once during his seven years
of imprisonment—from 1897 to 1904—for a period of
seven months he was not permitted even to lie down.
Several of his friends were executed, and in a Korean
newspaper he read the notice of his own death.

Young Rhee believed that his name was next on the
list of those who assuredly were to die. As he faced death
he found that none of Korea's ancient religions—Shaman-
ism, Buddhism, and Confucianism—spoke a clear word
about a future life, but he remembered that Christianity
did. Through a released prisoner he sent word to his old
Confucian father to smuggle a New Testament into the
prison. Then while Rhee was bound in the stocks one
prisoner would stand guard at the door while another held

the little Testament open before him and turned the leaves.[3] As he read day after day he at last found light and finally accepted the Christian faith. He then began to speak to the other prisoners and even to the keeper of the prison. The latter, like Paul's Philippian jailer, was finally converted and baptized. Though Rhee was under sentence of life imprisonment, the jailer now took him out into the large hall, where Rhee daily conducted a Bible class of forty adults, including the jailer. Five centuries previous, one prisoner had ironically called this awful dungeon the "Hall of Blessing," and now in very truth it became just that for these political victims of the old Emperor. There began in that prison a revival of religion, from which finally emerged a score of Christian leaders, both statesmen and evangelists, who were to build the new Korea.

In 1904, with the aid of his missionary friends, Rhee was able to leave Korea and continue his education in America. There he took his B.A. degree at George Washington University, his Master's degree at Harvard, and his Ph.D. at Princeton. At the latter university he became the ardent disciple of Princeton's president, Woodrow Wilson. During the Japanese occupation of Korea, which began in 1905, Rhee, with a price upon his head, attended a meeting of Korean exiles in Shanghai where he was elected the first President of the Provisional Government of a free Korea. Upon the liberation of Korea on October 16, 1945, Rhee returned to Korea after thirty-five years of exile during which he had spoken all over America and Europe on behalf of Korean independence. When he came to

---

[3] I have long had that Testament in my possession and have promised to return it to President Rhee when I go out to Korea again in 1955.

Seoul General Hodge personally introduced him at a mass meeting of fifty thousand people.

Dr. Rhee was the first elected national Korean leader in more than three thousand years of Korean history. In July, 1945, as the head of his party "For the Rapid Realization of Korean Independence," he was elected President. He was strong enough to get Parliament to alter the constitution to provide for the popular election of the President and then to be elected President again in 1952. At one time he spoke to me quite casually, as President Masaryk of Czechoslovakia had done toward the close of his own life, of the possible necessity of his own crucifixion in the presidency.

However serious his faults, he is fearless and stubborn enough to stand alone against the world. On our last visit I found Dr. Rhee the same old friend, affectionate, humble, and utterly informal, unspoiled alike by his long years of imprisonment, his forty years of discouraging political campaigning as an exile, and his sudden elevation to high office. It is still too early to pass final judgment upon him or to assign his place in history. Sometimes he has seemed to do the right thing at the wrong time and in the wrong way. When he released the prisoners of war, many of whom had never been in action, he did what we should have done two years earlier, as Walter Lippmann pointed out. If by careful screening we found a number who would rather die than return to Communist hands in China or North Korea, we should simply and quietly have released them. Instead, as innocent as babes in the wood, we tried to make Russia lose face by reporting faithfully every name, with the implication that we would be prepared to sacrifice thousands of American boys rather than return these prisoners. Whatever the unknown future may hold, up to the present time Korea has seemed to be the land of American mistakes.

Lack of space does not permit me to record my observations of the revolutions I have witnessed in other countries —such as Israel. Each revolution is significant in itself, but the fact that practically every nation of the Near and Far East is caught up in revolution is even more significant.

Chapter 10

MEN I HAVE KNOWN

To travel for sixty years in a world often torn by war and revolution has sometimes meant physical discomfort but has always meant adventure. For one thing, it has brought me into contact with many of the great personalities of my generation. The rich friendships of life have been to me one of its most precious assets. What a host of glorious people there are in the world!

All my life I shall be glad that I heard Caruso sing. My old scrapbook also reminds me of hearing Adelina Patti and Jean and Edouard de Reske. I saw Edwin Booth play Iago in *Othello* and later Henry Irving in several Shakespearian plays. I shall always be glad that I talked with Bernard Shaw, incomparable satirist and most brilliant conversationalist I ever met. Once when we met Shaw at Lady Astor's he was introduced to Helen Keller, and he wounded her with the flippant remark that he had supposed all Americans were deaf, dumb, and blind. I am glad to have seen Christy Mathewson pitch, Honus Wagner in the infield, Ty Cobb play his incomparable game, and Connie Mack's "greatest team of all time." I recall the football stars of the same generations; Heffelfinger and McClung were in my class at college.

Among the men of destiny Stalin is indelibly stamped
on my memory as he stood on Lenin's tomb reviewing a
great sports parade of youth clad in flaming colors and
marching with wild enthusiasm to their massed bands.
Standing with him were Maxim Gorki, the leading Soviet
writer of his day, and Maxim Litvinov, Foreign Minister.
I had known the more brilliant first Foreign Minister,
Chicherin, a man of less moral earnestness than Litvinov.

Stalin always seemed to me to be deeply suspicious of
everyone, perhaps the result of two decades in prison and
exile, of being hunted and hounded by the Czarist police
and finally arrested by one of them who he thought was a
fellow Communist. He was cold, ruthless, cruel, crafty,
motivated by implacable hatred of everyone he faintly
suspected of ever having opposed him. He really believed
in a secret police and made sure that he had all the information—or misinformation—needed to put to death
any enemy. He was an able general, a master politician,
silently planning his every move on the political chess-
board while the more brilliant Trotsky was out commanding the Red Army and making eloquent speeches. Stalin
believed himself to be a true Marxist, a loyal follower
of Lenin, and a man of destiny who alone could save
Russia; therefore, in his mind all the purges, mass mur-
ders, and slave labor camps were justified.

I shall always be glad that I saw Hitler as he arrived
at the Kroll Opera House to make his "blood bath" speech.
I heard him boast of having killed a multitude of men in
that purge of his enemies which advanced his "revolution
for power." Hitler was a finer-looking man than I had

expected from his photographs and he had certain remarkable gifts and abilities. No one could dominate the able generals, the industrial magnates, and the masses of German people without unique ability. He was not a wholly malignant devil who had sprung full-grown from the brain of Satan. No man seeks or chooses evil for its own sake but always for "the apparent good." Hitler was only the spear point, the symbol, the embodiment of the evil of the time. Human psychology being what it is, someone had to try to revive the greatest warrior nation in history. Someone had to protest against the evils of the Versailles Treaty with its false statement of the "sole guilt" of Germany. The fact is that the Allies, including the United States, and Germany were all guilty before, during, and after the war, even though Germany's guilt was the greatest.

A disorganized but powerful mind is revealed in Hitler's *Table-Talk*. His promised New World Order seemed a possibility for a time and lured the Germans to follow him—to their doom. His hatred of the Jews, resulting in his destruction of six million of them, was one of the most demonic facts in history, the more despicable because as an unemployable neurotic he had formerly been fed in free soup kitchens of Jewish philanthropy. But at this point only those entirely free from anti-Semitism can cast the first stone.

I am glad that in my own country I knew the last two of the men whom I consider our five greatest Presidents: George Washington, Thomas Jefferson, Abraham Lincoln, Woodrow Wilson, and Franklin Roosevelt. I realize that this appraisal will immediately raise emotional resentment in some people. We must recognize, however, the American habit of maligning our living Presidents, making each a scapegoat, while we place upon a pedestal our great dead.

I met Woodrow Wilson in the White House after my return from China, where I had just seen Yuan Shih-kai. While Wilson had obvious intellectual and moral qualities that were lacking in the old pagan war lord, Wilson himself was deficient in some of the rich personal qualities that Yuan possessed; for Yuan reminded me a little of the more winsome Teddy Roosevelt. Wilson was the scholar in politics; Plato's philosopher in the modern Republic. Though he seemed cold and infinitely reserved, there was something of moral greatness in his character. He was a moral Puritan, a "Presbyterian priest" who would have felt at home in Calvin's theocracy. As Wilson interpreted the war to the people of America and the world, his state papers rose at times to the highest level of those of Jefferson and Lincoln. But, like Herbert Hoover, he could not work with an opposition. He counted his opponents "wicked wilful men." Lloyd George told me that the last time he called on Wilson in Washington, when Wilson was a broken, dying man, Wilson could not even then forgive his enemies. Whatever his faults, he was one of the few men I have known in pulblic life whom I would call really great. When I asked Lord Lothian, who as Lloyd George's private secretary had daily observed Wilson in action he said: "In all American history I would place Abraham Lincoln first, George Washington second and Woodrow Wilson third."

Franklin Roosevelt I met three times. In his portraits

his profile shows his strong and stubborn Dutch jaw, but this was never obvious in his presence for he was graciousness personified. He lacked the intellectual stature of Jefferson and the moral earnestness and bedrock integrity of Lincoln; yet judged by what he did in the depression following 1929, in World War II, and in the sweeping reforms he undertook, I believe history will be compelled to rank him among our five great Presidents. Practically all British statesmen agree with this judgment.

When one of our American Seminars visited Washington we met members of the cabinet and Congress and other outstanding individuals, but no one impressed us more than Mrs. Roosevelt. The venom and scorn with which she was viewed by her political enemies was the result of false propaganda. Of those who really knew her there was almost no one who did not think highly of her. She had none of her husband's faults and possessed many virtues that he did not have. She has been held in high honor by all members of the United Nations except for a few cynical Russians.

In India, Lord Curzon was the most brilliant of all the Viceroys I saw and Lord Halifax the greatest saint among them. He, and more especially Lord Cecil, had a humility and a rare tenderness seldom found in men. Lord Haldane and Lord Sankey were both gentle mystics, one a philosopher and the other a fine legal mind. I never saw convincing evidence of the intellect with which both were credited, as I did in Sir Stafford Cripps, who was, however, lacking in political sagacity. At many points there was a strange resemblance between Cripps and Woodrow Wilson.

In England, I found Lloyd George more brilliant and facile than Churchill but lacking in his Scotch-granite integrity. Still, Lloyd George's genius led and saved Britain in World War I—which the nobler and gentler Asquith and Grey could not do—and Britain owes him a lasting debt of gratitude. Lord Balfour, Lord Asquith, Lord Grey, and Lord Haldane, all on the cabinet with him, were finer characters, but only Lloyd George could save Britain in that hour.

I saw him first in the House of Commons when he was a rising young Liberal lawyer and a member of the cabinet of Henry Campbell-Bannerman. Later when he rose to genius as War Minister and then became the famous war Premier, he was so magnetic that his very presence was mesmeric. He moved men and led them, often against their wills. In preparing an address he collected his facts by consulting every expert and authority, pumping them almost dry, then mastering these facts before he faced the Commons. He was eloquent, persuasive, commanding, courageous, inflexible in the pursuit of his objectives. When it came to winning the war, he towered above Kitchener and all the generals. But he cracked at his seam of greatest weakness—his moral character.

To Lloyd George politics and war were both stupendous games to be won at all costs and by any means. As a joyous pagan he seemed not so much immoral as amoral. In certain abilities we would have to go back to Pitt to find his superior, but he finally lost the confidence of his country and of his own Liberal party. England is generous, however, to its benefactors, and even members of the opposition are given an honored place as elder statesmen in the House of Commons, a recognition that is not awarded in America.

Lord Baldwin was a friendly personality and a Christian gentleman but his lazy drift meant an undefended Britain. Indeed, it was almost an unarmed Britain which he left to the cold Chamberlain, who flew with his umbrella to seek peace at any price with the thundering Hitler. It was only Churchill's Cassandra-like prophecies that then awoke sleeping Britain. I saw Ramsay MacDonald presenting a brave and handsome front as an orator in "his Majesty's opposition," but he was a pathetic example of Lord Acton's dictum that "all power corrupts" after he had betrayed the Labor party for his own ambition and later when he was degenerating visibly as Prime Minister.

Clement Attlee, whom I have known for years, is a gentleman and a scholar, respected by all, but one would have to ransack the world to find a man who could make a poorer speech on the occasion of some important national crisis. Neither he nor Thomas Jefferson could make a moving speech. It is the more remarkable that Attlee was such a reconciler in holding together his cabinet, including so many powerful personalities.

Aneurin Bevan is the only labor orator whom Churchill hesitates to meet. Such radicals have a way of seizing power in the crises of history. However, cold-blooded Britain, never hysterical, never stampeded, is less vulnerable than most countries. We must, however, always keep an eye on Bevan and never underrate him.

Harold Laski annually gave our Seminar the most brilliant lecture of anyone in Europe. He was not as great a

soul as R. A. Tawney or Sidney Webb, and would sometimes sacrifice a truth for an epigram. But after reading
the beautiful correspondence between the aged Justice,
Oliver Wendell Holmes, and the scintillating young genius,
Laski, I can see that he had humility and tenderness in his
heart which he never showed to an audience. How little
we know of each other, after all, and how utterly incapable
we are of finally judging any man.

The most towering statesman of our generation is undoubtedly Winston Churchill. A grand old warrior, he is
always longing for the front, for he would rather fight
than eat. He has not the military genius of his ancestor,
the Duke of Marlborough, but he is a far greater character. He is a master of words and possesses the finest literary
style of any military man in history. Although he was the
savior of Britain in the war, in the time of unbelievable
poverty through which Britain was compelled to pass he
was not a great Prime Minister, for he had an economic
blind spot resembling that of Herbert Hoover.

Coupled with Mott, the master organizer, was Robert
E. Speer, a spiritual giant. His was the most winsome
personality and the most Christlike character among the
student leaders of the last generation, and he moved us
all to the depths when he spoke to Christians. He was
deeply reserved and seemed to feel he could not invade
the personality of others even to be an effective evangelist,
as could Mott. His life was wholly Christocentric, and the
personal gospel was so complete and satisfying to him
that he never seemed to see or be able to proclaim a social
message. His character and message resembled the tenderness of the prophet Hosea rather than the thunders

of judgment of Amos. Speer's gifts perfectly supplemented and balanced those of Mott.

Among the leaders of religious thought in America Reinhold Niebuhr has proved a prophet of disillusionment to our times, and like the prophets he has been counted a pessimist—which he never has been, only a realist. There seem to me to be four main strands in his thought: first, Christian orthodoxy, derived from St. Paul, Augustine, Luther, and Calvin; hence his emphasis on sin and grace. He can hardly be classed, however, with the "neo-Orthodox" or with Karl Barth. Second, modern liberalism. As a result of the scientific spirit and historical criticism, modern liberalism derived from the Renaissance and the Enlightenment. Though a thoroughgoing liberal, Niebuhr is one of the most merciless critics of the futilities of modern liberalism. Third, Marxism. In his social theory, Niebuhr has been influenced by Karl Marx but he is also a scathing critic of Marxism as a total interpretation of life. Fourth, balance of the individual and the social. In his social gospel Niebuhr is not a naïve optimist like Rauschenbusch, whose aim was "to establish the idea of the Kingdom of God in the thought of the church and to assist in its practical realization in the world." Niebuhr is one of the few who keeps a complete balance between an individual and a social emphasis in Christianity, between optimism and pessimism, and between religion and culture. With his leaping intellect and piercing insights he has made the most brilliant addresses to which I have ever listened. He is more brilliant and more influential than Paul Tillich, who, however, is a more profound philosophical theologian. Niebuhr is rapid and impatient and has seemed to many proud, but I have always found him a humble Christian, a fearless prophet, and a true friend.

The life that was the most dramatic and romantic among my friends was that of Raymond Robins. Although a gold seeker in Alaska, he found not gold but God. After that tremendous experience in the far North, he and his cultured young wife settled in the "bloody seventeenth ward" of Chicago and for some twenty years fought to make that mighty metropolis a clean city. Against him in the battle for Chicago were such gangsters as Al Capone, such plunderers as T. Yerkes and Samuel Insull, and the poison press of Hearst and Colonel McCormick. With him in the fight were Governor John P. Altgeld, Harold Ickes, some of the great merchants, such as Cyrus McCormick, and professors in the University of Chicago, such as Charles Merriam and later Paul Douglas. It was from Robins' lips that I first heard "the social gospel," as it was then called, before I ever heard Walter Rauschenbusch or Washington Gladden.

In 1917, on a Red Cross mission to Russia, Robins saw Lenin found his revolutionary government and frequently had to deal with Lenin and Trotsky in political crises. He was the greatest labor orator, sharing honors only with William Jennings Bryan, probably the greatest political orator of his day. Although I had admired Bryan in many ways I was ashamed of him when I heard him bitterly attack evolution before an intelligent audience in Scotland. I knew Robins in his beautiful home in Florida when he was lying on his back, broken from a fall while pruning trees on his estate. With his courage still indomitable, he told the story of his recollections of Bryan, Theodore Roosevelt, Hughes, Hoover, Harding, Coolidge, William Allen White, and other great figures of his day.

It has been said that a man is never a hero to his valet—but I find no obstacle to the valet's (or secretary's, or junior fellow worker's) becoming the hero! Such has been my experience, for a number of my assistants have become heroes to me. When I first met Kirby Page he was a poor boy from Texas, a "root out of dry ground." But I watched him grow into an indefatigable student, speaker, and writer. In my judgment he has become today the most powerful pacifist in America, or probably in the world. As a speaker and writer he has been deepening the spiritual life for thousands. I would not for a moment suggest that he could ever be considered a candidate for the Nobel Peace Prize—that munitions money should be reserved for such pacifists as General Dawes! Although Kirby Page may not aspire to move among the worldly great, some humbler and much more effective work for a new social order he is certainly doing.

We have been affectionate friends and co-workers for more than forty years. Together he and I have tried to use the three techniques employed by all the great social movements, whether organized by Wesley, the abolitionists, or the Communists, our opponents. All such movements have sought to preach their truth by the spoken word to individuals, to groups, and to the multitude. All have used the printed page for the distribution of inexpensive or free literature; Kirby Page and I when together produced and sold over a million copies of pamphlets and a hundred thousand copies of books. And third, all the movements have believed in the organization of like-minded people, first into intimate groups and then into national or international bodies.

I was privileged to have a remarkable succession of private secretaries, and I have been proud of the work of every one of them. Among them Bromley Oxnam, later Bishop of New York and Washington, was one of the ablest. He has been a fearless exponent of the social gospel, especially in Washington, where we need his witness to the Christian conscience. I am very proud of the work he is doing in exposing the un-American action of Congressional committees. Pat Malin, another secretary, is now doing priceless work as secretary of the American Civil Liberties Union, in an hour when all our liberties are threatened.

From time to time I have met individuals above the plane of our common humanity. Of these men Einstein impressed me as having the greatest intellect. He is obviously a genius. Like Tagore, he is a beautiful creature.

Among these mountain-peak individuals were seven of the most Christlike characters I have ever known. As I write there lies before me an old copy of the New Testament, now worn and falling to pieces although it has been bound and rebound many times. On the flyleaf of this little book I have at some time asked each of these people to write his or her name. The list reads: M. K. Gandhi, C. F. Andrews, Amy Carmichael, V. S. Azariah, Toyohiko Kagawa, Syngman Rhee, and Albert Schweitzer. Of these, two were Indian, two English, one is Alsatian, one Korean, and one Japanese; six were Christians and one a Hindu; four were from the Orient and three from the Occident;

but none is an American. We have led the world in most material achievements but not in the making of saints. As I have already written quite fully concerning Bishop Azariah I will pass on to add a brief word concerning the others.

Charlie Andrews I knew when as a brilliant young Cambridge scholar he came out to St. Stephen's College at Delhi. Andrews fell ill and was nursed back to health by a young English Baptist missionary who also substituted for him in teaching his college classes. When the situation was reversed and his young Baptist friend lay ill of fever, Andrews wanted not only to nurse him but to take his church services also. This, however, was not in accord with Episcopal sanction nor permitted by high Anglican practice. Regretfully therefore Andrews felt it necessary to give up his orders in the Church of England and went to join the poet Tagore in his college in Bengal and dedicated himself to universal human service.

Wherever in the world a great catastrophe occurred, whether famine or flood, slaughter or racial conflict, there Andrews went and turned the searchlight of publicity on the situation. Several times he barely escaped prison. He always moved freely and fearlessly, equally at home with oppressed Indians or Negroes, with Viceroys and Prime Ministers. In his combined gentleness and boldness he was not unlike Francis of Assisi or Gandhi, his closest friend. I knew and loved this man for thirty years. It was the sheer overwhelming nature of his love that caused thousands of Hindu and Mohammedans all over India to say that his initials C. F. A., really meant Christ's Faithful Apostle.

Amy Carmichael came from the Keswick school of evangelical religion in England. She first went out to Japan as a missionary but shortly afterward broke down and was ordered home, in her own eyes a complete failure. As she regained health she determined to see if she could stand the tropics of India. During some sixty years she never returned home on furlough and ended her triumphant service in her beloved India. Early in her work in that country she began to rescue the little girls who were being sold or given to the Hindu shrines for lives of temple prostitution. She not only rescued several thousand of these beautiful children but turned the people's attention to the temples as houses of prostitution. Miss Carmichael had the most beautiful and Christlike character I have ever known. In my early days in India we lived under the same roof when I was studying the Tamil language. I once asked her the secret of her living, and she told me that it had begun in a meeting some decades previously when one sentence in a prayer had transformed her life—"Thou art able." Since that time she had been living one day at a time in simple faith in the encompassing sufficiency of God. I can witness that I have never seen any other person live so triumphantly by faith.

Kagawa, who might be called the Christian Gandhi of Japan, was the son of a Japanese official and the adopted son of a rich uncle who drove him from his luxurious home the moment he indicated his intention of embracing Christianity. His father had died as the result of dissipation and his elder brother had had seven concubines. His family for three generations had been maintained only by geisha girls and such women. He himself, the son of a concubine, went to school with a feeling of shame, and when he heard the story of Jesus the Carpenter of Nazareth, who poured out his life for the poor, it gripped the heart of this young idealist.

During his course of study Kagawa contracted tuberculosis. He decided that if he had only a short time to live he would have his kind of fling before he died; so he chose to go into the slums of Kobe, inhabited by some twenty thousand outcasts, paupers, criminals, beggars, and prostitutes. During the thirteen and a half years that Kagawa lived there the slum was thrice stricken with plague, five times with cholera, twice with dysentery, thrice with smallpox, and every year with typhus. I saw the place where he lived on two dollars a month in a little room six feet square without a bed, without a stove, without a table or a chair. Sharing his mat with a beggar he contracted chronic trachoma. Five times he was arrested for his fearless vindication of the rights of labor, for he was both a labor leader and a founder of co-operatives.

Kagawa is a prolific writer, a novelist, a poet. In all, he has written more than fifty books and pamphlets, and more than a million copies of his works have been sold. His religion is at once personal and social. He believes that we must Christianize society and socialize Christianity.

Albert Schweitzer stands deservedly as one of the famous men of our time. When he was perhaps the most brilliant young philosopher and theologian in Germany, as well as one of the outstanding organists and an authority on Bach, he turned his back upon all his achievements, studied medicine, and went as a medical missionary to bury his brilliant life in the abysmal need of the African tropics. Even there he cannot be hid, for the eyes of the world are upon him. And from his hide-out his authoritative volumes of philosophy continue to come. His whole life is a vicarious ministry to the Negro, who he believes has been wronged by the white race, and a testimony to the sacredness of human personality.

I have reserved Gandhi for final mention. I count Gandhi the greatest personality I ever met and the greatest saint on earth during our generation. I can quite understand why Kagawa when he came into Gandhi's presence fell on his knees. I know of a score of men like Vincent Sheean and Louis Fischer who have felt his influence just as I did.

Gandhi seemed to combine three contradictory men in one: Gautama Buddha, the gentle Francis of Assisi, and the rational revolutionist Thomas Jefferson. Only late in life did Gandhi recognize that he was a man of destiny, confronted by three seemingly impossible predicaments. First, how could he instill in the hearts of four hundred millions of the impoverished, illiterate masses of India the deathless determination for liberty that burned in the hearts of Washington, Jefferson, and Patrick Henry? Second, how could he, without striking a blow, free them from the rule of Britain? Britain, the strongest empire in the world, possessing a great navy, army, and air force. Britain, many of whose leaders felt with Winston Churchill that they would rather die than let India go; they had won India by the sword and by the sword would hold her.

Third, even if freed, how could he unite India, the most divided country on earth; how could he help forge a constitution that would weld Indians into one brotherhood and make the segregation and further oppression of sixty million untouchable outcastes a crime?

These three impossibilities Gandhi achieved despite the fact that for years he seemed to be the incarnation of the inferiority complex of his whole subject people. Like Abraham Lincoln, during the first years of his life Gandhi seemed to himself and to others almost a complete failure.

He was born October 7, 1869, in the little seacoast town of Porbandar above Bombay, where his ancestors had been Prime Ministers of a tiny Indian state. As a boy he was slow, hesitant, shy, with a sensitive mind and conscience. His three years' study of law in England were years of "misery," shyness, angularities; he suffered from his utter inability of self-expression, and when he failed in Latin he had spells of brooding depression.

In 1891 Gandhi returned to India hoping in time to become the Prime Minister of his native state. In his first lawsuit he stood silent and stuttering and lost the case through his inability to speak a word. At the age of twenty-four he went out to South Africa as the lawyer for a rich Moslem to collect a debt of some $200,000. There he saw the indignities suffered by his 150,000 fellow Indians under indentured slavery. He collected his debt and, when begged to stay in South Africa and help the dispossessed fight their battles, he remained for twenty years. While he thought he was trying to free 150,000 Indians, in reality he was learning to overcome all fear in life, including fear of the foreigner, and was unconsciously preparing himself ultimately to lead to freedom the four hundred million impoverished people of India.

In South Africa he was "kicked, beaten, spat upon." When imprisoned, sixteen thousand of his fellow Indians, awakened and emboldened by his example, came forward seeking imprisonment with him. Gandhi issued a tiny sheet called *Indian Opinion*, as insignificant as Lenin's tiny *Spark* or William Lloyd Garrison's *The Liberator*. Quoted throughout the Indian press, however, Gandhi's spark set India ablaze. At Delhi the Viceroy, Lord Hardinge, presided at mass meetings of protest against the injustices in South Africa. In England Lord Curzon and Lord Ampthill, former Indian Viceroys, addressed Parliament and the British people; while Lloyd George, although he cared little about Gandhi or his fellow prisoners in Africa, did not want to lose India, where public opinion was already seething, so he brought pressure to bear upon General Smuts in Africa urging that the Indians there be granted their demands. After twenty years of agitation, imprisonment, and suffering, Gandhi won his battle, set his fellow Indians free from their worst indignities, and started back to India.

Gandhi was forty-six when he returned to India in 1915; he was probably the most disciplined man on earth and the man with the greatest spiritual power. He was God's instrument to free India. For a year he silently surveyed the injustices India was suffering, then chose his battlefields. The government had put a tax on salt so that the poor were hit below the belt. He decided to march to the sea to take God's salt from God's sea and give it to God's poor. He marched with his barefoot followers, took the salt, gave it to the poor, and then went to prison as God's voluntary prisoner. The hearts of long-oppressed millions, however, rose in new courage.

Gandhi next selected the Bardoli taluk, or county, under the leadership of the great Patel, as the place in which to lead the peasants in civil disobedience, in refusal to pay their land tax, an act whose results might have left the Indian government without adequate income. But before Gandhi could organize this radical step, three times in other parts of India his undisciplined followers under severe provocation broke into violence. Gandhi said sadly: "India is not yet ready for non-violent revolution" and went back to prison himself. This broke the heart of the impatient Nehru and his fellow prisoners but Gandhi held them back for two more decades until India was finally ready for independence.

Gandhi chose the voluntary fast as his most effective weapon. I remember once during a time of fighting between Hindus and Moslems when he fasted for twenty-one days in penance for their violence. On the tenth day the doctor, feeling his fitful and feeble pulse said, "His heart is failing; he will be dead by tomorrow if he does not take food." Gandhi opened his eyes and said, "Have you forgotten the power of God?" He was stronger on the twenty-first day than he had been on the tenth. When they carried him out, too weak to walk, the Hindus and Moslems had stopped killing each other and again Gandhi had won the object of his fast. He called for his Hindu brother to read his favorite passage of Scripture, his Moslem friend to pray to the one God and Father of all, and then his dearest Christian friend, C. F.

Andrews, to sing his favorite hymn, "When I Survey the Wondrous Cross."

In 1947 communal riots broke out between Hindus and Moslems in both India and Pakistan; a million victims were killed and twelve million refugees driven homeless across both countries. Gandhi then entered upon the last of his thirteen long fasts. The same year, in the providence of God, both Britain and India were at last ready for political separation. Lord Mountbatten was sent out as India's last Viceroy to hand over the government to India's free republic under the long-imprisoned Nehru as Prime Minister.

Gandhi had his Judas, a bigoted Hindu named Godse who wanted to kill Gandhi and wipe out a few million Mohammedans that there might be a pure Hindu raj. On January 20, 1948, Gandhi came to Birla House [1] in Calcutta for his daily prayer meeting. He arrived a little late; Godse spoke to him, advanced, bowed before him, and then fired two shots. Gandhi fell, folding his hands in prayer and exclaiming, "O God."

Gandhi's signature given me on December 3, 1929, and a photograph which I took of him in his ashram at the same time are before me as I write. Above my desk hangs his large portrait. They remind me of the last time I saw him at a meeting of the Congress at Lahore that year. Fifteen thousand people were gathered in the great tent when Gandhi moved his resolution for the complete independence of India—after asking in vain for forty years

[1] Birla was an Indian millionaire. In December, 1929, I sat on the floor at dinner in Gandhi's ashram at Sabarmati between Gandhi and Birla. I was told that Birla had already given half a million dollars, or half his fortune at that time, to Gandhi's projects designed to free India.

for Dominion status such as Canada enjoyed. Gandhi sat on the platform not ten feet from me, too feeble to stand because of his weak heart.

After I left the huge Congress meeting I went over to Gandhi's little tent to say good-by. Outside I saw a crowd of a thousand or more simple illiterate peasants and wondered what they were doing there. Gandhi told me that he had one last word he wanted to speak to the throng in the great tent, so we started to return. Then I realized why the crowd was there. Once in a lifetime, they were waiting to see him as he passed by! Because of the railway, newspapers, telegraph, radio, and all modern means of communication at least ten times as many people had heard of him and wanted to see him as had ever heard during his lifetime of Gautama Buddha, more than twenty-three centuries earlier, or of Confucius in China; more than had ever heard of Moses, or Isaiah, of Jesus, or Mohammed. I saw mothers hold up their children as he passed, children who would be told in later life that they had seen Gandhi with their own eyes. I saw educated men close their eyes, fold their hands in prayer, and stoop to kiss the dust from his aged feet.

At one time I spent ten days with this great man and as I sat beside him and discussed many questions I came to realize that he believed with his whole heart in nonviolent revolution through vicarious suffering. He had first learned this principle from the Sermon on the Mount. Gandhi, a joint product of Hinduism and Christianity, was the unique handiwork of God. We all knew that he might die in one of his fasts, or upon some cross in vicarious suffering, yet I felt that he would never die, that he would live and India would be free.

Some who do not understand Gandhi will object that I have given him space out of all proportion to the other men I have mentioned, but I believe he was wholly unique. I class him among epoch-making men such as Gautama Buddha, Zoroaster, Confucius, and Mohammed. Though he did not found a new religion he was more deeply spiritual than any of these others. George Washington freed three million colonists from mighty Britain after seven years of war. Gandhi freed four hundred millions from the same Empire without striking a blow.

I have mentioned but a fraction of the significant men I have known—political and spiritual leaders and friends. What men they were and are! What a world of great men are all about us.

Chapter 11

❦

THE SCIENTIFIC METHOD
IN RELIGION

Life for me has been a strenuous adventure not only in witnessing the revolutions that have swept over the world
but in the revolutions in my own inner life. One of these
was caused by the introduction of science and the scientific
method. My first experience with this method was with
my beloved professor William Rainey Harper, while still
at Yale before he went to found the University of Chicago.
I shall always be grateful to Dr. Harper for opening my
eyes to the principles of evolution and of historical criticism. There was a certain shock, but also a thrill of adventure, as Dr. Harper showed us that the stories of creation,
the tower of Babel, Noah's ark, and the flood had all been
written in Babylonia centuries before they were repeated in
the account of Genesis. In Babylon the stories were based
on a pagan polytheism with no ethical content whatever, while in Genesis we read: "In the beginning God
created the heavens and the earth." Man is made in God's
image, capable of spiritual fellowship with him. There is
a world of difference between Genesis and the myths of
Babylon.

For me the Old and New Testaments contain the word

of God, but they are written in the words of men. No
inspiration can make Mark's crude grammar equal Luke's
flowing Greek, or the Fourth Gospel equal to the first three
in historic accuracy, however deep its spiritual insight.
There is neither infallibility nor verbal inspiration in the
flat contradiction between the account of Judas' death in
Matthew 27:3–10 and the account in Acts 1:18, 19. In
the former, Judas hanged himself and the priests took his
money to buy the Field of Blood: "Then was fulfilled
what had been spoken by the prophet Jeremiah." There
is no such verse in Jeremiah; though thirty pieces of silver
are vaguely mentioned in Zechariah 11:13. The account
of Judas' death in the Acts represents a contradictory tradition. These passages are typical of many others. Just as
the Bible is not verbally infallible, neither is it morally
infallible. A Moloch-like God depicted in Revelation who
would endlessly torture his helpless victims with no hope
of reformation or redemption would be a cruel and immoral God.

It is frequently a painful process for a student coming
from a fundamentalist home to make the transition from
a traditional to a rational and vital faith. Many never
make the transition at all, but lose their rationally incredible faith altogether. For me it was a joyous release
from bondage of "the letter that killeth," to the glorious
liberty of the free sons of God. I had no more need of an
infallible Book than of infallible parents. I agreed with
my dear friend John Dewey at this point that the quest
for absolute philosophic certainty was forever vain. I was
now a candidate for truth—all truth.

Many of my adventures have been in pioneering in dangerous or unpopular fields. To become a herald of the social gospel and demand justice of selfish capitalism, or to urge equal brotherhood without segregation in southern colleges and churches, or to demand peace in a warring world as it enters the atomic age are all adventures in controversy that are painful unless one becomes a bit tough and really loves a fight. Finally, when I tackled the most unpopular cause of all in investigating psychic research, I little realized that I was entering one of the greatest adventures of my life. I felt I must find out if there actually is sufficient scientific evidence to support belief in survival, or personal immortality, or whether such belief is purely a question of blind religious faith.

This quest was instigated, in a sense, in 1937 when my devout Quaker friend, Edward C. Wood, felt a "concern" to ask me to investigate psychic evidence for survival. I told Mr. Wood that I was already fighting on too many fronts and had neither the time nor the interest for more. He said that if I wished *I could have direct evidence of the survival of human personality after death.* He told me he knew of various gifted persons who were in touch with two worlds, the material and the spiritual, the visible and the invisible, and he immediately introduced me to several of these gifted persons. From 1937 for the next thirteen years I quietly made an unhurried investigation of scientific or psychic evidence for survival. I had the advantage of travel on three continents and I kept records of all the evidence I received.

I did not agree with Gladstone, who considered psychic investigation "the most important work in the world—by far the most important." But I observed that many of the leading men in England who had formed the Society for Psychical Research in 1882 were far in advance of us in America in this investigation—Arthur Balfour, John Ruskin, Lord Tennyson, Alfred Russel Wallace, Lord Rayleigh, the Bishops of Carlisle and Ripon, Sir Williams Barrett, Sir William Crookes, F. W. H. Myers, Robert Louis Stevenson, Conan Doyle, and Sir Oliver Lodge. As I look back upon my experience I think that, providentially, I was particularly fortunate in coming into touch with some of the most powerful psychics, and of being preserved from the painful ordeal of fakes and frauds of whom I had a horror.

Out of a hundred sittings during these thirteen years may I select one that was typical of many. On April 16, 1938, I went to meet my friend E. A. Macbeth in his apartment in the Ansonia Hotel, New York. Macbeth was a businessman who owned the water works at Rhinebeck, New York, and I never knew him to make any charge for his psychic work. Among his many psychic gifts the most satisfying to me was that of the "direct voice." His "control" in the other world was "Father Tobe," who, as Tobias Emerald McCarthy, had been a Doctor of Philosophy and a member of one of the Roman Catholic orders in Ireland and who had died at Elizabethtown, Kentucky, on April 2, 1852, which he called his "birthday" in the other world. I am glad that I have myself no psychic gifts whatever, but anyone who was not stone deaf could hear Father Tobe's rich deep voice, like a Russian bass or a grand organ. His character and intelligence always reminded me of

Gandhi's and I never asked him any question in philosophy or theology to which he did not have a rational reply.[1]

On this evening of April 16, after opening with the Lord's Prayer and several familiar hymns, Father Tobe spoke to us—some fifteen persons—for about half an hour and, as far as time permitted, answered all our questions.

Among others who spoke to us was my son Arden, who had passed from this life on April 17, 1917, at the age of fifteen. He talked to us and answered questions in his own clear voice for about twenty minutes. My father then came through and spoke to me for about the same length of time and referred to his last day in the tent with us when we were deer shooting in Colorado in September, 1894.

The actual circumstances of my father's death were these: as receiver of the Missouri, Kansas and Texas Railway he had put the railway successfully on its feet, but the job had cost him his health. We were foolish to have gone to an elevation of some twelve thousand feet for our camp in the Rockies. On September 4, I had gone out for the early morning shooting and when I returned found my father alone in the tent. As I was then preparing to go out as a missionary to India, I got out my New Testament and began to read it for my usual "morning watch," without realizing how lonely my father was. He said, "Read aloud, my boy." I read the whole of the fourteenth and fifteenth chapters of John. Then we discussed those "many mansions," which must have seemed wistfully near to him. That night when I came in from the evening shooting all

[1] My friend Macbeth, himself, knew nothing of philosophy or theology. His personality was utterly unlike that of Father Tobe; he could never have answered our questions or met our cross-questioning on such subjects.

were sitting round the roaring campfire laughing, talking, and eating venison. My father sat next to me on my right. Suddenly I heard a sigh and as I turned, his head fell forward and he passed instantly away. There was no pain, no parting, no deathbed scene.

That evening in April, 1938, I was eager to learn from my father how he knew when he opened his eyes upon a new scene that he had "died." My father said: "I passed over, due to the high elevation which was too much for my weak heart which had suffered from overwork on the railway. I did not realize at first that I had 'died,' as you say on earth, until I met my old friends, Bass and Kellogg, the latter an engineer of the railway." As soon as my father said "the railway," hoping to get something evidential, I said: "What railway, father?" He answered, "The Katy." (As we had traveled over the Missouri, Kansas and Texas Railway in my father's private car, we had always affectionately called it the "Katy," as others did.) I had never heard of Mr. Bass or Mr. Kellogg, so this could not have been taken from my mind by telepathy. Later, when I asked my uncle, who was the claim agent of the M. K. & T., he told me that Kellogg was a civil engineer, responsible for keeping a section of the railway in repair.

When I asked my father concerning our last morning in the tent, he said we were reading together "the Scripture." When I asked, "How is mother?" he replied, "She is as dynamic and aggressive as ever, and consequently she had a rather hard time over here at first, but she always was a wonderful woman." When I asked him about his work over there, he said: "I always was an organizer and I am organizing over here, working for others. Your mother, Margaret, and Arden are with me here. Dana also is over here, but not with us here at the moment. We watch the progress of little Arden there with you; he is a fine boy. I am with you very much of the time, more than you would believe if I told you."

After my father, some twenty persons "over there" spoke to their relatives, including Dr. Frizell, whom I had known as a former president of Hampton Institute, Virginia. He was speaking to his daughter, who was sitting in our circle, and then quite unexpectedly called my name and gave me a personal greeting.

On my right was sitting a bacteriologist who had known and worked with Surgeon General Gorgas and General Leonard Wood, when they were fighting yellow fever in Cuba and in the Panama Canal Zone in order to build the Panama Canal. I was hardly listening to the conversation of others, thinking only of my father's words, when General Wood's voice, speaking above us, turned from the bacteriologist to say: "I remember you, Sherwood Eddy." I replied, "I remember you, General Wood, and our conversation as we were sitting at a baseball game in Manila, when you were Governor of the Philippines. I remember what we both said when big George Kelly, first baseman of McGraw's New York Giants was at bat, but I was only one of thousands you saw in the Philippines and I did not think you would remember me."

The whole evening was an evidential one, as the voices of a score of people, all different but each speaking in his own recognizable voice, came through to us for three hours, while the psychic, Dr. Macbeth, sat among us in silence. So far as I could learn, no single mistake was made in any of the messages. Everyone present seemed to be as completely convinced as I was of the reality and genuineness of the voices and of the personalities of the departed who were present. Much of the material was intimate, evidential, and quite beyond any information Macbeth might have had. Such experiences were repeated for me in various parts of the world for more than thirteen years.

As I look back over the years in which I was seeking evidence in this country and abroad, my experiences of psychic phenomena were—with one or two exceptions—so repeated, so convincing, and so satisfying to me personally that I can say that *I now have the same evidence in principle for the existence of the nine members of my family who are now in the spiritual world that I have for the three members who are still on earth.*

Yet evidence that was firsthand for me becomes only secondhand for my friends or readers, some of whom quite naturally want firsthand evidence of their own. And that is just what I cannot give. I think the evidence was first opened to me because I needed it when I was speaking to the fighting men and others who had not enough religious experience of their own to be sure of survival. I have recorded much of my evidence and findings in my last book, *You Will Survive After Death.*[2]

I would advise the average man to leave the subject severely alone unless he finds some psychic of undoubted integrity. We have to leave some things to experts; we cannot make our own independent experiments in explosives, atomic bombs, X-rays, and many other fields. At

[2] Published by Rinehart & Company, New York. I have had more gratifying responses from this book than from all of my other books combined.

best I find the whole psychic area a "twilight zone," and I quite agree with Georgia Harkness in her recent article that "the evidence thus far adduced is inconclusive," so far as the majority are concerned and I think it will continue to be so.[3] At first hand it is sometimes overwhelming; at second hand it is inconclusive and unconvincing.

For me this study of survival has been a great adventure. I no longer think in terms of "one world" in time, but of one universe with its many inhabited worlds in eternity. It is my Father's universe, at once my battleground and my playground. But I am convinced that most of us Christians must accept the hope of eternal life on faith: "Blessed are they that have not seen and yet have believed." It may not be intended that we have sufficient scientific evidence for any of the great ultimate realities. It cannot be an accident that the proof—or disproof—of all the great finalities lies forever beyond the reach of man's proud reason. Neither by science nor by philosophy can we prove before the bar of cold reason the existence or the character of God, the fact of survival, or of personal immortality, the resurrection of Christ, or his relation to God. I doubt if one can prove to the satisfaction of every member of a class in philosophy either one's own existence or that of one's own mother.

Tennyson says:

> For nothing worthy proving can be proven,
> Nor yet disproven.

[3] *Religion in Life,* Winter, 1952–53, p. 85. Dr. Harkness writes: "Even where such data are seriously accepted by persons of some intellectual standing, as in the case of William James, Sir Oliver Lodge, and currently Sherwood Eddy . . . the evidence thus far adduced is inconclusive."

But we do not need scientific or philosophic proof for any of these things. We can know God with such satisfaction and assurance that we neither need nor desire any pale philosophic proof, which would not add to the sunlight of our assurance. We can have life at this moment, so real, satisfying, and abundant that it will give us a rocklike faith and the "sure and certain hope" that it will vastly increase. All these things we may have in our own experience.

My years in psychic investigation have brought me in touch with many of the great "cloud of witnesses" to personal immortality. I came to know Stewart Edward White in his trophy room of big-game shooting in Africa; Upton Sinclair and his psychic wife, Ozora Davis of the Chicago Theological Seminary, who had many psychic experiences; Dr. Edgar Brightman, who investigated the subject, as well as the scientific investigators of Duke University, Dr. William McDougal and J. B. Rhine. I began finally to realize that a practically unbroken chain of witnesses to psychic realities has existed ever since Croesus, King of Lydia (560–546 B.C.), initiated the first instance of successful psychic research.[4] It included a long line of medieval saints such as Joan of Arc (1412–1431), Protestants such as George Fox, John Wesley, and Swedenborg; Alfred Russel Wallace, Daniel D. Home, Frederick W. H. Myers, and Air Chief Marshal Lord Dowding, who directed the Battle of Britain against Hitler's overwhelming air force, and who told me in his club in London of his

[4] I was moved in the summer of 1954 to visit Delphi in Greece, where the psychic oracle of Apollo had used telepathy to tell King Croesus what he was doing at the moment. We motored through Galilee past Endor, where Samuel had denounced Saul, saying that he would be defeated by the Philistines on the morrow and the kingdom would be taken from him.

own convincing psychic experiences with his beloved airmen who had been shot down.

I did not realize while making this investigation what a radical change of outlook it would give my thinking in terms of this one mighty evolving universe, with its multitude of inhabited planets which may be among the "many mansions" prepared for God's children in their eternal growth and spiritual service. Certainly my investigation of this "twilight zone" has resulted in one of my greatest spiritual adventures.

Chapter 12

❦

WHAT I BELIEVE

I n this statement of my beliefs I claim no originality, for like Sir Isaac Newton I "stand on the shoulder of giants." It is not necessary, however, to use quotation marks because it will be quite evident what and how much I owe to my beloved friend Reinhold Niebuhr, to Paul Tillich, William Temple, and more recently younger men like Nels Ferré.

I have no formal creed, or closed system, nor is there a single historical creed that I accept in its entirety. I am sure that the quest for absolute certainty is forever vain and I shall never seek such certainty. I have no desire to be orthodox or "neo-orthodox," but neither do I have any aversion to being either. There is nothing I have to believe; I am free to seek truth.

God is doubtless absolute, but my life is everywhere relative and dependent and I have and need no absolute access to him. In the whole universe all is open. I find nothing closed, final, or perfect—neither the Bible, the Church, human reason, nor anything in the whole evolving universe. Everywhere I am under the aegis of relativity, but I am related to God and utterly and joyfully dependent upon him, who is the Source of all.

My essential credo is the shortest known, "I believe God." Yet it contains everything necessary to my sustenance and growth. The New Testament expands and explains this essential creed to read "God is love."[1] And this I passionately believe; it is the keystone of my arch of faith. The dynamic element of God's infinite love doubtless leads him forever to express himself in continual creation. And we may be able ultimately to understand the whole of experience in the perspective of this supreme faith that God is love.

"I believe in God, the Father Almighty, maker of heaven and earth." I believe he is not only all-powerful and all-wise but all-loving and therefore in the highest sense personal. I believe he is the only absolute, complete, and unlimited personality. Being itself—the source of our little fractional personalities, which are made in his image. God is not *a* person beside other personalities but he is not less than personal, for he is the ground of everything personal. He can initiate and respond to personal relationships and be in communion with all personal beings. I believe in God utterly transcendent though not "wholly other," and completely immanent, in whom we live and move and have our being.

As I grow older I become more and more theocentric.[2] I remind myself, however, of the words of wise John Calvin: "How can the infinite essence of God be defined by the narrow capacity of the human mind? . . . How can the human mind by its own efforts, penetrate into an exam-

---

[1] I take up the problem of evil in the next chapter.

[2] I Cor. 15:28. "When all things are subjected to him; then the Son himself will also be subjected to him who put all things under him, that God may be everything to everyone." Revised Standard Version.

ination of the essence of God, when it is totally ignorant of its own? Wherefore let us freely leave to God the knowledge of himself. For he alone is competent to witness for himself, being only known by himself."

With the whole Church catholic throughout the centries, however, I have found God and known him in experience in his threefold self-manifestation as Father, Son, and Spirit; God creating, redeeming, and indwelling; God as transcendent, Incarnate Redeemer, and immanent quickening Spirit, or God present in the heart—one God, *known to us*, not absolutely but relatively, in our rich threefold experience.

When I say that I believe that God is the maker of heaven and earth, I do not mean that he makes them as a carpenter makes a table, as things external to him. The first word of Genesis is a noble word: "In the beginning God created the heavens and the earth." Yet I believe that that statement was only a dim adumbration of the august spectacle of God, motivated by love, evolving the whole constantly expanding universe with its hundred million galaxies, nebulae, and island universes, by eternal and continual creation.[3] Under the modern dynamic theory of matter [4] we abandon the old idea of force as a relic of

[3] I have no morbid fear of anthropomorphism. I do not accept Pope's crude couplet:

"All are but parts of one stupendous Whole.
Whose body Nature is, and God the soul."

But if the body is our way of being related to the world, if it exists for the sake of communication and manipulation, and if it is the meeting place for selves, nature, and God, then I see no objection to viewing the whole electronic structure of the universe, visible and invisible, as in a sense the body of God.

[4] According to Becquerel, Roentgen, J. J. Thompson, Schroedinger, Einstein, Niels Bohr, and other modern scientists.

animism and leave forever the former crude materialism, to find matter and energy interconvertible. We find matter simply organized energy and energy matter broken down and released for work. We find no shred of materialism in a whole universe of mind. Yet we find an incalculable power hidden in every atom, so that man in his pride imagines he can blow up his little world and destroy it. Or, as was intended, as a fellow worker with God in his creative activity, man can in a humble way share in developing an evolving universe.

I believe God evolves the universe and that therefore the universe reveals God—in part and imperfectly, not exhaustively. God is so infinite that before him the whole visible universe is but a dim shadow. He is not *a* being beside others, not *an* object of thought whose existence can ever be proved or disproved by any rational argument. For God is always beyond both subject and object. He is the ground of my subjective self, of all existence, of all being, of the entire universe.

Apart from the universe, I believe there is an "abyss" of meaning and infinite potentiality in God that is not revealed in the visible universe. It is this infinite God who is our ultimate concern: it is this God whom we worship and this God who is love. Daily I declare my love in worship: "I would love thee, O Lord my God, with my whole heart, my whole mind, my whole might in service, my whole soul or self; help me to love my neighbor as myself." And just as in human love we grow by expression—for what is not expressed dies—so I find empirically that love for the Beloved, though never perfect, grows each time I declare it.

Because I believe in God I believe in man. I believe that man is made in "the image of God," capable of finding God and of fellowship with him. At the height of his being man stands before God at the juncture of nature and spirit. He is both free and bound, blind and farseeing, strong and weak, good and bad. At the depth and in the center of his being man is sinful. Sin begins in unbelief, in pride, in independence of God. Initially self-centered, man becomes selfish. The hard core of sin consists in making ourselves the center of life. Hence come lust and a whole brood of appetites and evils. The consequence of sin is the loneliness of a loveless life, a life "without God and without hope."

I believe that God was "in Christ reconciling the world unto himself." I believe that God entered human history in Jesus, the Christ, that in this one great deed of God, as a revelatory event, all history is forever centered and divided. Henceforth every event is either B.C. or A.D., before Christ or in the year of our Lord. All history thereby becomes significant and we are assured of the final triumph of God, either in history or beyond it. For God is not only in our little history of this minor planet but chiefly beyond it. He not only is immanent in time but inhabits eternity.

I believe in the incarnation, that Christ was very God of very God—and that Jesus was very man of very man. If he was really man, then I believe he was limited and fallible. Apparently he believed in a flat earth, in a world created in six days, and in his speedy coming on the clouds of heaven, as the Son of Man.[5] To me this evidence of his

[5] If all Jesus' followers, including the Apostle Paul, believed this, they probably received it from him. The last chapter of Revelation repeats the apostolic hope three times in the statement: "I am coming soon." R.S.V. Does "soon" or "quickly" mean nineteen centuries?

fallible humanity is very precious. I am content to be fallible and to have our Lord made like unto his brethen, if my Heavenly Father is infallible.

I believe that Jesus lived, died, and rose again from the dead. I believe that he was so identified with God that he was crucified for our sins. Herein is mystery, utterly beyond the grasp of man's feeble mind. I believe in the atonement, not a crude, crass "transaction" of a mechanical salvation to which I am asked to give easy intellectual assent. Perhaps the atonement was wrought out in the Being of God before the foundation of the world—*if* love needs any atonement. I believe that the cross is an eternally present fact in God as well as in history. Surely God cannot destroy evil except by taking it into and upon himself. I believe the atonement was achieved in history, visualized before us in Christ crucified. Perhaps it is symbolized or dimly adumbrated in our human experience in every parent who suffers for his child who sins.

I believe God, the Absolute, Eternal, Self-identical I AM THAT I AM, unknown and unknowable except in so far as he reveals himself, but truly known as finally revealed in Jesus Christ the incarnation of love. For knowledge of God can never be given in words or doctrines but only in persons, and supremely in One who is the way, the truth, and the life. Revelation is in some sense universal. I have found priceless truth in all religions by which myriads of men live. Yet I find the revelation in Jesus Christ unique, supreme, and final for our world.[6] The God-given nature

[6] "For God has other words for other worlds
But for this world, the Word of God is Christ."
Mrs. Hamilton King in *The Disciples*. Quoted with approval by William Temple in *Nature, Man and God*, p. 511.

of this revelation is emphasized by the fact that it is not dictated but must be discovered. God's revelation and man's discovery are correlative and reciprocal.

In his ever-expanding universe, continually God creates, God redeems, God rules and gives his "little flock" the Kingdom. All is of God. I believe that in God man is moving forward in his multiform life—economic, aesthetic, ethical—to inherit all truth, beauty, goodness, and love. Therefore literally all things are ours, whether the world, or the universe, or life, or death, or the present, or the future in this life and beyond—all are ours and we are Christ's and Christ is God's.

In my daily thought I am no longer concerned merely with "one world" but with *one universe*. This one universe God is creating, evolving, expanding, sustaining, and indwelling. I do not believe with Plato that God inhabits only a transcendent world above nature and above history; I believe there is one universe of things spiritual and material, invisible and visible. There is no clear division between the sacred and the secular, between the theological and the scientific. There is one universe, one Kingdom of God. I am heir alike of the Church catholic, the Reformation, and the Renaissance; in God I lay claim to all truth, all beauty, and all goodness.

I see one universe with its hundred million galaxies, star clusters, milky ways, and nebulae, and I firmly believe, with its thousands of inhabited planets, peopled by free, and therefore sinful, beings who must be redeemed. I see beyond this life not the monotony of heavenly harps—for the mighty symphonies of heaven will not be monotonous —but the adventure of worlds to be won by God and his fellow workers. We must graduate in thought not only from our earth-centered but from our sun-centered little solar system to our one God-centered, living, and expanding universe. Christ is God's unique revelation to *this* world, but must we believe that a life ending in crucifixion on this minor planet called Earth is God's only redemptive incarnation? Could not God be incarnate on each inhabited planet, working through prophets identified with the people peculiar to each planet, speaking to their own times and conditions? With John Calvin I am content to leave all these considerations to God. I believe that Jesus Christ is the Savior of humanity, although there is salvation in all religions, for it is God who saves. Since it is God who is the Savior of the universe, my ultimate theology is always theocentric.

Regarding eschatology, I believe in the ultimate triumph of God as sovereign in our world and in his universe. As the goal of all histories I believe in the coming of the Kingdom of God, beyond history. As the chief act of worship of my life, as I take the Holy Communion every Sunday morning on my knees, I believe that I "proclaim the Lord's death until he comes." I do not believe he is coming on the clouds of heaven, visibly, or to reign in Jerusalem, literally, but I am quite sure of the final triumph of God and of his Kingdom in the universe, on this planet and on every other inhabited planet.

I believe the wages of sin is death, in the sense of moral separation from God. I believe in the fact of hell as self-exclusion from the Father's heart and home, here or hereafter. I believe it lasts as long—and only as long—as God is excluded from man's life. But while it lasts I believe it is an awful fact—awful beyond the utmost ability of any genius to describe, Dante in his *Inferno* or Milton in his *Paradise Lost*. But if God is love in a moral universe, then hell, or self-exclusion from God, is not everlasting. I do not believe that finite sin in man's brief span of life merits infinite punishment, or that an all-loving God could eternally torture helpless sinners. If he did he would be infinitely worse than Hitler, who revived his victims in order to torture them a few more days. I believe in no monotonous, static heaven, in no permanent hell, in no eternal punishment, and in no personal devil in the dualistic sense which divides the mighty sovereignty of God. I believe, however, that there is still unfortunately an appalling amount of evil in God's spiritual universe.

There is no death. When we leave this outworn body the transition of passing through the portal to the larger and better life beyond does not end the eternal grace of God. He is always and equally the God of all grace, before and after death. To teach differently, to insist on eternal punishment taught in an infallible Book in this rational universe, is to create rebels like Shelley, who cried:

> Is there a God? Ay, an almighty God,
> And vengeful as almighty.

I find myself in far greater sympathy with Shelley and a host of fellow rebels in all centuries than with some of the harsh Christian fundamentalists. I recall one such fundamentalist in India who, when I told him that I believed Gandhi was among God's "other sheep not of this fold," tried to have all my meetings throughout India canceled because I did not believe that Gandhi must burn in an everlasting scriptural hell.

I rejoice that Nels Ferré and Karl Barth, neither of whom seems as yet to have a closed system or a closed mind, "seem to be turning to a universalist doctrine that in the end all are saved." [7] If God is love, if it is not his will that any should perish, if Christ died for the ungodly, then given all time and eternity, all power and all love in God, may it not be literally true that "we have our hope set on the living God who is the Savior of all men, especially of those who believe" (I Timothy 4:10)? There are many passages contradictory to this one, but so there are contradictory passages on all other essential doctrines. In any case, I hold to this hope of universal salvation.

I believe the Bible is a record of God's revelation to man. That it contains for me that revelation is evidenced by the worn-out Bibles on my desk. With the Pilgrim John Robinson I believe that "yet more light is to break forth from God's holy Word." God has many things to say to each of us but perhaps we cannot bear them now. There is not one of us but who is crude and imperfect in character and equally so in cultural development. I am ashamed of much that I have done; I am more ashamed of what I have left undone; but most of all I am ashamed of what I am, at eighty-four years of age. Yet I am not discouraged.

All of this life is but the first round of the fight. I have never been knocked out, and I shall live to fight another

[7] Daniel Day Williams, *What Present-Day Theologians Are Thinking* (Harper & Brothers, 1952), p. 118. Also my own *You Will Survive After Death,* p. 160.

day. I cannot say, "I have fought the good fight; hence-forth a crown." But eagerly I expect to enter the second round of a far more strenuous fight, not for "one world"— our one little earth—but for one mighty and ever-expand-ing universe. Relative to this larger life beyond, most of our experiences to date have been limited; they are but the dim outskirts of God's ways. What no eye has seen, no ear heard, nor the heart of man conceived, God is prepar-ing for those who love him.

I have no closed system but I must end, as I began, with my surest, most central and certain conviction: "I believe God." With Isaac Newton I still feel that I have been "like a boy playing on the seashore . . . while the great ocean of truth lay all undiscovered before me." "Now I know in part," yet "*I know Him* whom I have believed and I am sure" of the future. I am assured of the future because in the past he has faithfully—yes, literally and almost mirac-ulously—kept his promise for body, mind, and soul. I can trust him in the great beyond in time and eternity, for he ever fulfills his promise, on which I rely every day of my life: "God will supply every need of yours according to his riches in glory in Christ Jesus."

Chapter 13

❦

THE SECRET OF HAPPINESS

I f I have learned anything in more than eighty years of life, I believe I have learned the secret of happiness, and it is a secret that is richer when shared. Happiness is something which everyone desires but few find. Happiness is not an end in itself; it is an all-important barometer to indicate whether one's relationships with life are right or wrong. Happiness is not something that can be sought and found, for if we seek happiness we never find it. Jesus did not say, "Seek first happiness and you will find it." With infinite wisdom he said, "Seek ye first the kingdom of God and his righteousness"—then all things, including happiness, shall be added unto you. With somewhat the same thought the wise Kant said, "Seek not happiness but to be worthy of happiness."

Happiness is never found in outward circumstances which are beyond our control, but in inward attitudes which are within our control. This is a fortunate condition for a generation like ours which has known so many events that do not make for happiness: the devastation and slaughter of two world wars with the hunger, depression, disease, and displacement that have followed them; and now the ever-impending destruction of atomic war. Yet the most radiantly happy souls in history have lived in times that were worse than ours today.

Before we begin to discover some of the secrets of happiness we must come to grips with the dark, basic realities of life, especially the problem of evil, the fact of suffering, and the mystery of pain. The problem of evil has always been the hardest question man has had to face and the heaviest burden he has had to bear. It is our common problem; no one escapes it. It is the problem of all religions, all philosophies—in fact, of all mature men, even if they are not conscious of having any religion or any philosophy. Epicurus, writing some twenty-two centuries ago, well states the dilemma for all time: If God wishes to prevent evil but cannot, then he is impotent; if he could but will not, he is malevolent; if he has both the power and the will, whence then is evil?

Even if we seek to escape the problem by the hypothesis that there is no God we have not avoided the problem of evil; actually we have created a fresh problem: how then account for all the good—the truth, beauty, goodness, and happiness—in the lives of many? Obviously the darker realities of life have to be fitted into the entire picture of life, not denied, by-passed, or railed against. I was first forced to face the problem of evil and suffering seriously when I was working with the fighting men in World War I. When men are hourly living and dying in the reality of sin and suffering, the very air is saturated with their quest for a satisfying philosophy, as witnessed by their scores of questions night after night. One Sunday morning, while Kirby Page was my secretary, I dictated the whole book

Suffering and the War,[1] for use among the soldiers in the camps.

Many volumes have been written in an effort to deal with the problem of evil, books such as *The Theory of Good and Evil*, by Dr. Hastings Rashdall, in which he says: "Whatever evil exists in the world must be supposed to exist because it is a necessary means to the greatest good that the nature of things makes possible. . . . God should be regarded as willing a Universe that is the best that seems possible for a mind to whom all the possibilities of things are known, and who wills the existence of all that is actual because he knows it to be the best."

Summing up the convictions of many keen thinkers, we arrive at the conclusion that moral character is necessary to happiness, and that the achievement of moral character demands the fulfillment of six conditions: some genuine freedom of volition on man's part; some power of accomplishment in the direction of his volition; an imperfect but developing environment; a sphere of laws; a community of life—men living as members one of another; and the necessity that the individual struggle against odds for his progress.

These conditions are the price of moral growth. If, with Omar Khayyám, we would shatter to bits this sorry scheme of things entire and then rebuild it nearer to the heart's desire, could we improve upon this world we are in? For instance, would we sacrifice freedom of the will for the fetters of fate? Would we exchange the joy of accomplish-

---

[1] It was published by Longmans, Green & Company, in 1916, and circulated among the troops in paper covers as *The Meaning of Suffering*. Since it is long out of print I feel free to quote from it.

ment, with all its striving, failing, stumbling, and sorrowing, for a garden of delights fitted for lotus-eaters and dreamers? What kind of environment would we create for imperfect men? Surely God was wise when he matched man and man's environment; both are imperfect, and the very nature of imperfection means mistakes, which are synonymous with suffering and pain.

Again, if we remolded the world, would we eliminate order in the universe and trust our lives to the endless interferences and special miracles of capricious whim? Would this substitution bring more or less suffering to the world? When we do not co-operate with the physical and moral laws of the universe we suffer the consequences; but how infinitely more disastrous would be a world without reliable law! Such a world would be a chaos, not a cosmos, a madhouse rather than a maker of moral character.

Further, would we exchange the community of living— understanding, sympathy, mutual helpfulness—for isolated existence? But good human relations are possible only for responsible, disciplined human beings; and responsibility and discipline are loaded with pain and mental suffering. And lastly, would we omit the struggle and heroism of life through which, as Carlyle shows, "the dullest day-drudge kindles into a hero"?

Perhaps we may conclude that God's world is better than any we could create. I have come to the conclusion that all suffering is temporary and that most of it is manmade and removable. Also I have found that the suffering that cannot be removed can be resolved into three chief forms: disciplinary, remedial, and redemptive. Disciplinary suffering is a stimulus to man's development; remedial suffering is the result of man's own sin; redemptive suffering is voluntary and vicarious, borne for the reclaiming of men and the making of a better world. Shelley sums up the experience of the great sufferers, and indeed the philosophy of suffering, when he says:

> Most miserable men are cradled into poetry by wrong;
> They learn in suffering what they teach in song.

Savonarola suffers for the liberty of Florence; Huss burns for Bohemia; Livingstone lays down his life for Africa; Father Damien becomes himself a leper that he may save the lepers. William Prescott, almost blinded by an accident while in college, "sang aloud in his darkness and solitude with unabated cheer." With the help of others he mastered many volumes in foreign languages and completed his *Conquest of Peru* and *Conquest of Mexico*. But his greatest work was the conquest of himself. Thus, at last, for the Christian who sees the meaning of Christ's cross and accepts his own, time is conquered and his crown is won.

We may now consider what I have found to be the conditions of happiness, the criteria which must be met, the *musts* of endeavor: Recognize with Aristotle that normally *happiness is found in the harmonious exercise of function.* Every man has one, two, or five talents—save for a few rare geniuses who may have ten. Geniuses are seldom happy, for happiness is found not in the multiplicity of one's talents but in the use one makes of what he has. Whatever your gifts may be, use them in the service of all, for the happiness of all.

Normally, *happiness is found in health and growth.*

Jesus went about seeking to make men whole in body, mind, and soul. A sick mind often causes a sick body. Both need a cure; first the mind, then the body. Wholeness and health are normal and ultimately the will of God. But a sick body is sometimes necessary as the means of curing a sick soul. Just as health is normal, so growth is natural and imperative, for body, mind, and spirit. I must ask myself constantly, though never anxiously, "Am I growing?" That is why, with Browning I must welcome each rebuff that turns earth's smoothness rough.

Come to grips with reality, with the seamy side of life, with the problem of evil. Evil is not something to be explained away, but it can often be driven away. It cannot be removed by philosophy but often can be overcome by loving labor and sacrifice. Concerning each affliction I can ask: Is this suffering possibly disciplinary, remedial, or redemptive? If I will scrutinize my suffering I can often discover that all of it is a possible means to greater good.

Accept your limitations; fearlessly face the facts of life. All lives in this world are imperfect. When a person has made an honest inventory of his strengths and his weaknesses he has brought his life into perspective and neither boasts of his powers nor whines about his limitations. Happiness demands honest inventories with no counts taken under the influence of drink, drugs, or other illusion-building devices. In accepting the facts of life, accept the fact of death. If death is a foe, then it is a conquered foe, for God has delivered "all those who through fear of death were subject to lifelong bondage." Once you have faced the temporal fact of death and have seen through it, you will find that literally there is no death. It is only the golden portal that leads to the infinitely better life beyond. On both sides of the portal there is only life—here, often in limitation, pain, weakness, and suffering; there, in ultimate radiance, infinite growth, and triumphant gladness.

Conquer all destroyers of peace and fulfill the simple means of happiness. Fear, anxiety, and worry have a vicious influence, while faith, hope, and love possess revitalizing powers. Faith is the first condition for advancement in life whether in science or religion and usually holds the key to happiness. Hope means more than shallow optimism. Hope springs eternal in the human breast because God and his whole evolving universe are essentially good. Hence our highest hopes will be more than fulfilled in God. But "the greatest of all is love." Plato discovered this fact, as did Gautama Buddha long before him. Mo-tzu in China preached mutual love and denounced war; and Gandhi in India discovered that love is stronger than hate. I believe that love is the greatest thing in the world because God himself is love.

Happiness may be realized under many conditions and in many places, but I believe the best soil for its growth is in the home. Forgive me if I speak too frankly, but I believe that I have learned the secret of happiness in the home although I may not always abide by its laws. My wife and I say to each other frequently and fearlessly, "We are happy! We know we are happy and we are not afraid to be happy. We know why we are happy and we know how to keep happy." This realization does not come because we are perfect but because we are honest.

Both of us are working hard and continuously—sometimes overworking. When either grows tired there sometimes comes the quick, the impatient, the angry word; and love is wounded. If one nurses his sense of wrong, looking only at the fault of the other, peace is broken and happiness is arrested. There is only one remedy; one must confess where he himself was wrong. Instantly again leaps the upspringing fountain of life within! And "like a river glorious" the stream of love, joy, and peace flows on unceasing. This is happiness.

I see the world peopled with families. In their proper state people are not set apart as grains in "a loose heap of sand" nor compacted "in broad masses." They live in homes. Not the school, the church, the office, the union, the city, the nation, but the home is the basic, divine unit. All these other groups have their function but they are not the primary unit. Most of life is lived in a home and most of the lessons of life are learned at home. Here we must learn to live, or fail in living; here we must realize happiness or needlessly postpone it.

Marital love often begins in sexual attraction as the desire of persons for each other, but when it deepens in the life of a spiritual home we find that all love is rooted in God. Coventry Patmore once wrote:

> Love wakes men, once a life time each;
> They lift their heavy lids and look;
> And lo, what one sweet page can teach,
> They read with joy, then shut the book.

Why should we shut the book with one brief look and accept the dull monotony of life without continuing love, when a Divine Love stands ready to make each day of life pregnant with joy?

One does not have to know and analyze all the above conditions in order to find happiness. He will probably find in some one of these the missing link to his own life. It is fortunate for us, however, that happiness cannot be lightly found until the whole of life is rightly adjusted. It is life's great barometer.

Finally, all happiness for me stands or falls in the greatest adventure of all—the adventure of endlessly finding God. In finding God, one finds himself, his neighbor, and his hope for the world. In this discovery lies happiness. He comes to see the world in God and all history in God. Although God is so great that it takes a whole universe even to partially reveal him, and although all time and all eternity are his; still in his infinite love he is trying to help each of us to find the secret of happiness that lies even now within our reach.

Chapter 14

❦

RETROSPECT AND ANTICIPATION

As I look back over more than fourscore years, despite all my faults and failures life itself looks like one long glorious adventure. If I had it to do over again I would certainly do some things differently but I would undoubtedly make other mistakes, and I can think of no major choice that I would alter.

Through the years nine members of my family have been called to pass over into the eternal universe. They included our only son Arden and our daughter Margaret, who left her son, Arden Kerry Smith, my grandson. After nearly half a century of service with me, my wife, Maud Eddy, entered life in the unobstructed universe on August 29, 1945. Joyously I daily remember in prayer all the members of my family in the great Beyond.

On April 27, 1946, I was married to Catherine Louise Gates. She had served the Young Women's Christian Association in Toledo, Rio de Janeiro, and Montreal, and for seven years prior to our marriage was National Secretary of the YWCA in Canada. With her I have found the secret of happiness in joyous companionship.

The present finds us living in Jacksonville, Illinois, the community to which we "retired" when the tempo of New

York City became too fast and feverish for my advancing years. Here we find a delightful town with two colleges, three libraries, and fine people, many of whom play a good game of bridge. When one comes to retire he finds he is concerned not only with his vocation but with his avocations and recreation. One has to learn the art of growing old by keeping young. For me that means many interests, stimulated by wide reading, bringing out of one's "treasure what is new and what is old." One must cultivate interests in what is new without losing the treasured past.

Two years ago, like ten million of my fellow Americans I discovered that I have a heart. Speaking to a large audience in a church, trying to force my voice back under the galleries without a microphone, I developed a sharp pain, diagnosed as angina pectoris. I rested for a month and was all right again. Later, while entertaining an Oriental bishop, I foolishly struggled with his very heavy bag and experienced a second attack. I have had the advantage of the advice of the greatest heart specialist of whom I know in America, Paul Dudley White, of Boston. He allows me to do anything that does not leave me out of breath. I may dig in my garden, but I may not shovel snow ; I may climb steps, slowly ; but I must learn never to hurry, never to worry, and I must live without fear.

A slower pace means for me less public speaking—alas I can now take but one meeting a day—but more reading and writing. Now I can begin to make up for my lack of education in college by wide reading. All the recorded treasures of humanity, the wisdom, knowledge, and experience from the past, all of fact and of fiction are available for me to enjoy. Of course that means acquiring the habit of rapid reading and the selection of what is best, whether in stiff or light reading.

I found it a treat to begin with my Harvard "five-foot book shelf," every volume of which I enjoyed. When I came to Socrates, Plato, and the great Greek dramatists I had to digress to the history of Greece and an account of Greek literature, and then read Plato, Aristotle, Xenophon, Herodotus, and Thucydides. There were a score of similar digressions at the Renaissance, the Reformation, in science and philosophy, and in English and American literature. I can now make my own selections from some "hundred great books" and I am already well advanced in the tomes of Hutchins and Adler. If one cultivates a habit of good reading early in life, together with interests and avocations outside his business or profession, he has much to retire to and much to live for. With Emerson he learns to "live today," to live in the eternal present and never to postpone worth-while things.

One of my chief delights is the companionship of my beloved dogs, two thoroughbred boxers. These dogs I love for their sheer affection, loyalty, obedience, and companionship: they are never a problem, as human beings sometimes are, only sheer joy. I find more in the animal creation than I can put into words. Most men are so provincially isolated in human life that they never become acquainted with the whole hierarchy of beings in God's universe, both below and above man. Gautama and Gandhi in India, in fact the whole Orient, and Albert Schweitzer in Africa have seen more of God in the animal creation than we of the materialistic West have ever discovered.

I eagerly welcome the appearance of every important
book, such as Julian Huxley's *Evolution in Action* and
Fred Hoyle's *The Nature of the Universe*. I thrill at the
majestic spectacle of the whole evolving universe as I see
Hoyle's hundred million galaxies and milky ways, each
with over a million planetary systems like our own. I think
of the majesty of God, if in imagination I span our milky
way "a thousand light-years across." I do not see our
universe running down like a clock, or cooling off like the
frozen moon, but still expanding in the midst of eternal
and continual creation. New solar systems are continually
being brought into existence and sent flying out into space
at such tremendous speed that in time they pass beyond
the ken of even our present two-hundred-inch telescope.

I follow Huxley's two hundred million years from the
first primitive mammals to the one Godlike creature, man,
whose existence spans only "one-half of one-tenth per
cent" of the total age of our adolescent earth. I am not
alarmed if in less than ten billion years our earth will grow
hotter, will become a "red giant" and then a "black
dwarf" as dead as the frozen moon. Other planets are
cooling and ripening in this evolving universe to welcome
animal and human habitation. Professor Harlow Shapley,
Harvard astronomer, in his recent book *Climatic Change,*
describes the four ice ages on our planet, the last of which
was at its maximum 30,000 years ago. He thinks it reasonable to suppose that there are at least 100 million inhabited planets among the 100 quintillion stars of our
expanding universe.

I can lie in my hammock on a glorious spring day and
almost hear my beloved garden grow. I am quite oblivious

to the fact that we are hurtling through space at the rate of 700 miles an hour as the earth revolves on its axis, 70,000 miles per hour around the sun, and a million miles per hour around our galaxy! I feel not a breath of this dizzy whirl; I am in "the peace of God which passeth all understanding" as I dwell upon the marvels of his handi-work.

I am helped to understand our universe but not entirely satisfied in these writers whose works I am reading. Julian Huxley I knew personally in World War I as a gentle humanist. In his dim agnostic faith he thinks he can see in evolution a sort of "improvement principle" with a pos-sible trend toward progress. Yet, amazingly, "nowhere in this vast extent is there any trace of purpose, or even of prospective significance." The "possible progress" is the result of reproduction, mutation, and natural selection; nowhere does he see God! Rather I agree with William Temple when he holds that "The universe is a divine utterance; it grows more articulate at each state." Hoyle, while not a materialist, can find no religion in which he can believe, and sees Christianity as promising only "an eternity of frustration"—I suppose in playing harps in a monotonous heaven!

I am still more amazed as I read John Masefield's beautiful autobiography, *So Long to Learn*. As the result of his life's quest for truth and beauty he believes that "in the power and splendor of the universe inspiration waits for the millions to come. Poems greater than the *Iliad,* plays greater than *Macbeth*." But in his whole book the word "God" is not mentioned even as a pale hypothesis or possible explanation of the universe. It took John Masefield "so long to learn" to write his beautiful poems but I feel certain the day will quickly come—just beyond the great Portal of Life—when he will quote himself, "How dead I've been, how dumb, how blind" in failing to discover God. God was there, all through Masefield's life including those moments of psychic "inspiration" which he admits gave birth to his creative writing. God was eternally there, but perhaps Masefield had not kept open "the soul's east window of divine surprise."

I find myself closer to my friend Victor Gollancz in his recent autobiography, *My Dear Timothy*, and in his amazing anthology, which I have been enjoying under its English title, *A Year of Grace*.

Who can deny that Hoyle, Huxley, and Masefield have all found something, I would even say much, of God, though they do not, or cannot, or will not admit his name. I recall the "mystic experience" that John Dewey had when he was a young teacher in a high school in Oil City, Pennsylvania, with a "supremely blissful feeling that his worries were over," when he said to himself: "What are you worrying about, anyway? Everything that's here is here, and you can just lie back upon it. I've never had any doubts since then." What was this experience but a kind of inarticulate faith, that everything he needed was available—which I believe is true, but only true in God. Dewey had a faith for living that enabled him to be a great educator, philosopher, and social prophet. We only know in part and all of us are agnostic about many things; Dewey was a reverent agnostic about God. I need add only two words to Dewey's statement "everything that's here is here"—*in God*—and I too can just lie back upon him to supply all my need.

My days are filled with work, but my evenings are filled with the world's harmonies. In my new leisure time my greatest find has been a radio-record machine. A turn of the dial and I hear London, Berlin, Rome, or Panmunjom; another turn and I am in a former century with the classical composers of the past: Beethoven, Brahms, Mozart, Mendelssohn, Chopin, and Wagner. I hear the great voices of the past and present; Caruso, just as I heard him forty years ago; Pinza and Gigli, Flagstad and Traubel. I can appreciate now what my roommate in college, Sidney Lasell, did for me. He was the best pianist Yale had known for years, saturated with the classics, and as he played in the evenings we floated away into a world of harmony.

Every evening after the day's work we relax and enter into the eternal world of harmony and beauty. How I would like to hear some of the great composers— Beethoven when he is no longer deaf; Mozart no longer poor; Wagner no longer subject to degrading influences. In the Beyond they are surely still composing symphonies and operas amid the music of the spheres. And doubtless there are other composers there greater than these, as yet unknown to us.

At the age of eighty-two I thought of my work here on earth as nearing completion. But I have recently received an intimation which may be authentic that much may remain for me to do. Accordingly I am now spending some time in the midwest colleges and churches speaking principally on three themes: the present world situation, religious topics growing out of my spiritual pilgrimage, and the results of many years of psychic research, reviewing the scientific evidence of survival or personal immortality.

In the spring of 1954 with several friends I visited the chief centers of the Mediterranean—Egypt, Turkey, Greece, Palestine, and Italy. The journey brought us in touch with the four historic bases of our Western culture: the birth of our civilization in Egypt, of our culture in Athens, of our government in Rome, and of our religion of ethical monotheism in Palestine. For three months at the close of 1955 I plan to take another trip, around the Pacific, especially for evangelistic campaigns in Japan, Korea, and Hong Kong. Then I hope to return to America to continue speaking in the colleges and churches.

What of the future? It is only natural that the future which was opened up by my investigation of survival after death becomes constantly more vivid and real to me. I think I know exactly how the Apostle Paul felt as he faced the relative values of life and death—he did not know which to choose. I am eagerly ready to depart, to leap into the strenuous life beyond, "for that is far better." "But to remain in the flesh is more necessary" for the present. Frankly I crave every moment and every year that I can have here on earth with my wife, with whom I have found the secret of happiness. I have many duties yet to perform. I feel like an adolescent facing a challenging eternity. When daily I repeat the prayer that teaches us to pray, I say, "Thy kingdom come throughout the universe, on other inhabited planets as well as our own." Let me get beyond the brief and brittle egotism that is

only concerned with my petty self. Let me ripen to the
habitual, joyous appreciation of the work of all others.

> What matter we or they?
> Ours or another's day?
> Others shall sing the song
> Others shall right the wrong
> Finish what we begin
> And all we fail of, win.
> Ring bells in far off steeples
> The joy of unborn peoples.
> Sound trumpets, far off blown,
> Your triumph is our own.